PSYCHEDELIC NORWAY

Psychedelic Norway

John Colburn

COFFEE HOUSE PRESS
2013

COPYRIGHT © 2013 by John Colburn
COVER AND BOOK DESIGN by Linda Koutsky
COVER ART © Jennifer Davis
AUTHOR PHOTOGRAPH © Sarah Fox

COFFEE HOUSE PRESS books are available to the trade through our primary distributor, Consortium Book Sales & Distribution, cbsd.com or (800) 283-3572. For personal orders, catalogs, or other information, write to: info@coffeehousepress.org.

Coffee House Press is a nonprofit literary publishing house. Support from private foundations, corporate giving programs, government programs, and generous individuals helps make the publication of our books possible. We gratefully acknowledge their support in detail in the back of this book. To you and our many readers around the world, we send our thanks for your continuing support.

Coffeehousepress.org

LIBRARY OF CONGRESS CIP INFORMATION

Colburn, John (John Allen), 1967–
[Poems. Selections]
Psychedelic Norway : poems / by John Colburn.
pages cm
ISBN 978-1-56689-335-0 (Paperback)
I. Title.
PS3603.O417P79 2013
811'.6—DC23
2013003668

PRINTED IN THE U.S.A.
FIRST EDITION | FIRST PRINTING

this book is for Sarah Fox

ABSTRACT ORDER

FURTHER GEOGRAPHIES

Tonight when you go to bed
you must think
some very big thoughts.
Those big thoughts will make
your head grow larger.

—ARNOLD LOBEL
  Days with Frog and Toad

prelude

a brief tour of string quartet no. 3 by karel husa

1.

As a boy, Karel Husa began to cry and nothing could stop him. Not even a cloud. Not even a talking flame. He did not enjoy birth; he felt reduced to human size. All the rats and mice in Prague came forth from his tears. He pictured himself as a rock or a steaming kettle or a god. He continued to cry. His cries became music.

I will be your guide. Everything I'm saying came from these four rooms. How can you know if you are a constant size? You have to trust the room.

Karel Husa placed bandages on the earth. Those bandages rose to the sky and became birds, a sudden storm, a driving wind like a river in the air. He discerned no difference between feeling and sound. The bandages helped him avoid misunderstandings.

To understand the first room, consider: what does a ghost pull out of its chest?

You entered this room by listening to it. What you can see is not important. For example, birds trapped here try to spell a name. The name is you. Feel around for a bird. Address yourself with this motion. Imagine this: four birds try to spell all the names in a room. When I say *feel around* I mean *listen.*

You see a ghost pull a bird out of its chest. It sets the bird on the floor. The new bird walks around. Try to understand this room.

As a boy, Karel Husa began to make trees. They were easy to climb. They were made from sounds.

We drum on this earth all our lives; now we must sit down and listen. We are here because it is forbidden. This is just the first room.

The birds in this room make four sounds. Whenever one bird sings, the room fills with light. Whenever another bird sings the eyes forget. Shall we recollect our proper mission? We are here to obtain new feelings by listening. Another bird sings exclusively by waking up. It's a small sound. Whenever the fourth bird sings, you are in the wrong place, please step to the left.

As a boy, Karel Husa learned to handle arrows. They burned the air. They brought home a song's head, piece by piece. He placed bandages on the earth where these arrows fell, and the bandages flew up. One tribe of birds has only heads, one has only wings, it is confusing. Listen to how the four sounds change, according to wind blowing through the buildings of Prague. Then there is the bird pulled from the ghost.

The first room contains evil spirits to be used for food. In Prague Karel Husa often disappeared, only to reappear five steps later as a deer. The fires of Karel Husa rise out of distant caves. It is confusing.

In this room, one must eat like Karel Husa. Who does not understand? My name is listen. This is just the first room. Before you walk into any room you might die. Have you forgotten this? The bird pulled from the ghost is silence. That's the secret of the first room. Shall we move on?

2.

Try to arrange yourselves aesthetically. Notice how night falls like
a thick old bottle. Outside the trolleys sound dangerous, correct?
Notice how the second room seems to be built over a canyon.

Our tour continues: Karel Husa once picked up a pen in this
room. He put some flowers inside the pen. He grew the ink. He
wrote this song. Birds ate the flowers. Do you see?

The second room makes a slow breath happen around us. Rain
falls around corners here. Keep looking. You are in this room for
a reason.

Karel Husa built an altar in each corner of this room. Each altar
invoked a voice. Each voice lives in this song, as do we.

Another voice is also the voice of the bedroom door, but that's
nothing. We have to keep thinking about the room or it withdraws
beyond human events.

Notice the white paintings. Aren't they like sacred ears? That's
called interpretation.

If we consult the documents, we see a territorial passage here. We
see that insects rejoice. A dead fish floats by. Karel Husa invited
this frequency and it passed through the elements. If we move
carefully, if we step over the souvenirs, if we refrain from rubbing
or anointing, if we listen to what is woven into the room, we
arrive at an initiation.

In this room, the legend of Karel Husa emerges like a forehead. The legend drinks from a pit. The altars are governed by the question, and the question is governed by the voice.

Has your voice fallen into disuse?

We may ask about the circuit of the will. We may be touched and pronounce the name. Remember, he became Karel Husa by thunder, by a sudden calling. In this room we resemble each other. We become members of a secret.

My recommendation is to ask a question at each altar. My recommendation is to voice.

Do you have the sense that this room is being built as we think of it? At times you may have to crawl across. When I say *keep looking* I mean *listen*. A voice will come to you.

This room falls through space, like anything. The voice does not mention it. Shall we?

3.

Now the questions begin. You'll know because the body hollows out. That's how questions start. The third room may be a train. Clocks appear on the walls. We call that rhythm.

The word *now* may be deceptive in relation to the subject. Notice how the sound here tries to prove that every disturbance of equilibrium is a fantasy. The celestial cycles right themselves, the next world passes through us constantly, maybe we change into a fish. Each disturbance is part of a larger harmony.

One example of a question: *Are we on a train?* Watch for motion in your thoughts. Other questions will emerge.

In the center of the room, the jar full of water becomes a listening device, a way to make sound appear from beyond the grave. We prepare for the inevitable. The other side of a jar of water is a question. From there, Karel Husa's music searches for us.

The third room operates on a kinship system. There may have been folk dancing here. Do you realize how many things are being born in this room? The onrushing particles?

Your task is to make a question. For example, *Are we lost?* This room is not the answer to the question, but the receptacle. The room holds the question, like the jar holds the water.

Listen. The hand tears in two and keeps becoming a bird. Do you remember? What if this room is the interior of a mountain? Listen for the place your question will live. Do you remember?

The rats of Karel Husa spring to retrieve his tears. When I say *remember* I mean *listen.* I also mean caress, hinder, chase, corner, attack. Each wall translates the sound. You should never forget the third room. Please step through.

Karel Husa gathers now at the entrance to other people. We are found in the third room expressing our solidarity. This is not the place where one amuses oneself.

For a while Karel Husa tried to become this door. Can you hear that? Remember, a question comes from the stomach, not the brain. Then the ceremony of opening your mouth.

Do you notice how the threshold of sleep has changed? How can you be sure you have not crossed it? You have to trust the room.

Note the insects. This is Prague, after all.

We are beyond the grave. When we leave this room we renew our mystical bond with the earth. Are you ready?

4.

Picture a sky full of stars; you've entered the fourth room. A silent film begins. Someone shaves an ice cube. Listen: here comes the future. We've been waiting for it, haven't we?

The problem with the fourth room is that it's broken, it ends. And we can't fly. Notice how another time leaps out. A smaller time. We're not exactly in darkness, right?

That's because electricity has a hard time passing through music. Generally, it goes the other way.

This is our last stop. After this room, no one can follow. Remember the bird in the first room? From the chest of the ghost? Silence is bigger here, near the end. We welcome the mindless giant.

But first, let's sing about this room. Let's be mountains in this room. Or air rushing over them. Whatever we had on Earth was like food we ate to get to this room.

Sorry, how did we fade into just air? I skipped ahead.

Karel Husa is now ninety-two years old. This room is forty-five years old. The pattern, it's made from antedates. Do you understand the word *now*?

Perhaps as a result of our hands love comes shimmering into each bird. Can you feel that? And don't you think maybe there's a fireplace somewhere? Have you noticed how each direction also makes a sound? Do you understand your sound?

Air from a bird, air from a fire. If you weigh fifty pounds in the first room, you weigh ten ounces more in this room. It's the silence.

Also, when I say *sound,* I mean *feeling.* When I say *wait* I mean *listen.* Do you understand?

The earth is smart like Santa Claus. This room is flesh and spirit. Karel Husa arranged your existence and your name. The earth receives us. No one sees what is in the air. Karel Husa composed everything in these rooms. Our eyes fall asleep. We welcome the mindless giant. We will remember. Correct?

pre-occupation

1.

Saturday morning I fought the poison of sleep.
Hands came through the small window next to the door.
I believed I had a metal contraption affixed to the roof of my mouth that restricted the
range of my lower jaw.
Later, I realized I did not.
I drank cold tea and ate crackers for breakfast.
Two blue herons walked in the swamp where the horse track had once been.

Rain and snow do not have a house to live in.
A fish does not have a house to live in but lives in a specific area of water.
A cloud lives wherever a cloud lives.
A hoofed animal has limitations these days.
Room 11 featured a dirt floor I covered with a black mat from Wal-Mart.
A suitable room.
To my left was Alan, Room 10.
To my right was Jones, Room 12.
The hallway made by a low wall was otherwise open to the elements.
Rabbits occasionally wandered through.

At the County Information Center I read a pamphlet titled *So You Want to Enlist in
the Armed Forces . . .*
It was illegal for me to enlist during the course of my probationary period.
I read a pamphlet regarding the etiquette of tourism.
It held the following recommendations:
  Never kick garbage cans.
  Speak kindly to prostitutes.
  Never stand and stare at any happening.
  Never ask an interesting-looking individual if he or she is an artist.
  Do not attempt to direct traffic.

The period of my probation was indefinite, pending yearly review.
A moth flew into my throat.
I began to cry.

I was using myself up.
Some animal experts claim that pigs exhibit emotions, including shame.
I walked the corridors between various information centers, then to the inner district.
I sat near the Angel of Mill Park, disguised as a dangerous candy.
Birds were free to leave the county.
They followed migratory pathways in the sky.

"Hello," I said to the women who passed.
I said this politely, with my head bowed, a common practice.
One replied but continued walking.
I bought a day-old at the bakery.
People got mad.
They heard some music and started popping.
A jeep bounced into the curb and flipped over.
"All is well," I told the crowd.
The decisions an elephant makes in one day.
In one minute!

The bus station was near Mill Park.
We were legally required to wear orange shirts.
For the bus ride we covered these shirts with white coveralls, left behind at the Downs
by painters.

Orange showed through.
Five of us, spread throughout the seats of the bus.
I leaned my head against the window.
A man named Frank sat next to me.
Small eyes.

His vision swerved.

He held a paperback book.

It was illegal for me to visit a lending library.

2.

The countryside developed as film.
We saw burlap bags abandoned by the side of the road.
Frank's lips moved but no words were said.
He asked if I was going to the hanging and I said, "Yes."
I looked at the genitalia of the horses.

Frank said,
"I have money but I am studying to be a priest.
I renounce the ways of money by turn.
Weekends I am poor.
Let me read this to you:

> *Philosophies in relation can be encouraged to eliminate constructive outlets.*
> *The dignity of commercial traffic is the easiest kind of emotion.*
> *The movement will humor participation in decency.*
> *Men and women struggle with prosperity making a repetition of unevenly*
> *expressed reform.* "

I told him I was looking for a wife and he said he could not help me with that.
He had a wife and it seemed to bring mostly trouble.
There was a ruckus at the rear of the bus.
One of the men in my condition was trying to marry a young girl's photograph.
The bus driver made everyone exit into a field of tall grasses.
He told us he could shoot the troublemaker if we wished.
He had that right.
There were storm clouds.
We boarded the bus intact.
We could smell onions.

At the bus station, Frank attached himself to me.

It was evening.

He took the five of us for a meal.

"I have renounced all the latest things.

The action of the groin," he said.

We waited at the back door of a restaurant, in an alley filled with crates and boxes.

Frank passed fried chicken out to us.

Summer teased us.

Telephones rang.

Several not unamusing people passed us in the alley.

"We are torch singers.

How do you feel about Greenwich Village?"

We finished our chicken.

We had lead in our pencils.

Phosphorus in our bladders.

The antennas hummed.

Headlights made their discoveries along blank walls.

A shuttle took us to the hanging.

Everything was on Frank's money now, which he had renounced.

We saw many pilgrims along the road.

We became nervous upon nearing the prison.

A bell rang once.

This was not a time for musical experiments.

"Have your flashlights ready," said the bus driver.

It was not illegal for me to own a flashlight, though it was deemed "highly suspicious."

The hanging was to take place in the exercise yard.

One woman wore a shawl over her head and the guard made her remove it.

At the entrance gate we were informed that the yard was full.

No admittance.

I did not know what to do so I saluted, which later seemed like a suspicious activity.

Dogs circled the crowd, beautiful wild female dogs that had recently been pregnant.

I heard a rooster.

A man could easily split moonlight with an axe.

A butterfly is a rag blossom on tiny bones.

Frank bribed his way inside.

3.

To ride a bus is a gentle thing.
But I grew awkward in my seat.
The nature of pain is to make memory unattainable.
I saw the lives of insects ending on the bus windshield.
I didn't see the hanging but I heard the crowd moan in unison.
Word passed back: *The trap has opened.*
Then a moment later: *He isn't struggling.*
Then varied reports, all indicating that the hanging had been a success.

My coveralls were reasonably clean.
An atmosphere of completion prevailed.
Two men recited questions loudly across the aisle of the bus.
Out the dark window I thought I saw hides drying on the fencelines.
One man pierced the seat ahead of him with a tiny drill.

It was not safe at the bus station.
Our county seemed to have changed in the night.
The police were aggressive and I hid in the stalls of the bathroom.
Morning light began.
The fatigue of having a name, of answering a letter with one name, the equipment
                    required to live with these names, threatened on every side.
Civilization seemed a flimsy idea.
What hands are dragging the weights into darkness?
I had a series of untouched experiences.
I rolled up the coveralls and stuck them under my arm.
I walked home as people began to file out of their homes for church; my orange shirt
                    drew the occasional jeer.

Money is decorated for Christ here.
The hanged man saw no details.
Our political frontier is the throat.
I watched the rabbits.
Smoke drifted over the swamp.
I resisted the hands and their cups, their pleasure, the great heat of nailed hands.

I slept in the hot afternoon, conscious of clouds moving in.
I saw the hanged man in the swamp, walking in place with his chin up, wearing
                                                                    white coveralls.
When I woke, a man's hands pulled on me, dragging me from bed.
It was not unpleasant.
Out in the swamp rabbits ran in a strangely excited manner, knocking into one another.
Flames entered the hallway, some four feet high, I heard the sound of cooking.
In the smoke, all I could see were the orange shirts, and I followed.

We assembled in the swamp to watch the Downs burn.
Some firefighters came and made a trench.
I wondered if I could live off the land.
Feelings are on a wheel in the heart, is what I learned in elementary school.
Loads of black smoke drifted miles away.

4.

That night we slept on pallets beneath a canvas near the road, wrapped in blankets
                                                donated by the firefighters.
Some of the men had lost their orange shirts in the fire.
I woke at dawn.
I found a translucent bug on my arm, so small I almost couldn't see it.
I thought of the eroded face of the statue.
Alan urinated in the swamp.
He returned and said, "Jones is dead."

Our work that day required that both arms be raised above the shoulders continuously,
                                                for hours.
Cows nearby made sophisticated chewing noises.
The foreman held a tape recorder.
My shoulders felt as hard as pavement.
I heard an iron choir descend in the light.
The foreman threw a piece of brick at Gerry's naked back, it left a red scrape.
We worked too slowly, we were docked half an hour.
I had my orange shirt.

At lunch a television crew came to the tin shed where we ate.
A tall man with a microphone interviewed the foreman about our "pre-occupational
                                                program."
A pigeon flew into the cameraman.
They restarted the interview.
"Restriction of the willful body leads to a committed middle class.
Fatal emphasis on the command of character is not practical.
Our adults have carefully collected the standard obsessive qualities.
Life here is terrific."

We ate cold stew.

Our arms ached for pleasure.

The shy areas of our bodies drooped in the heat.

The foreman pushed the red PLAY button on the tape recorder and his voice came out of ▮

speaker:

> *lunch is now over . . . some people are still in prison . . .*
> *each of you is little more than an elaborate fungal system . . .*
> *you are not hungry . . . return to work.*

A group of crows had settled in a tree across the road from the shed.

As we walked down the gravel road, they flew up.

5.

Let us consider a representative sample of our population.
Each lone, unmarried man has a distinct preference for economic exchange.
One convict believes in a vocabulary filled with spirits.
Another has been seduced in public by the action of a tongue.
Still another's ancestors swam angrily and demanded clumsy embraces.
A new factor not mentioned is projected rage after marriage.
Each man accepts his future until it happens.
Each man's way of disregarding life is a habit from the era of his boyhood.

Let us consider the taboos of our culture.
It is generally forbidden, by unspoken consensus, to mourn death.
It is unmanly to wear gloves, though at certain jobs it is legally required.
It is acceptable to talk to ministers.
To play the radio is a form of religious skepticism.
Ownership of two goat's teeth assures a nightly visitor.
Any inheritances are apportioned by sexual rank.
It is unacceptable to indulge in the trappings of brilliant talk.

What traditions will survive the burning of the Downs?
The growing individual sheds superstition for the laws of society.
We returned to the pallets that night, with no word of available housing.
Two men were taken back to prison for not wearing the legally required
     orange shirts. They had broken laws.
There were fourteen of us left.
I slept between Gerry and Alan.
Rabbits jumped near the swamp as if to mate.
My black mat had melted.
As a child I believed that frightened birds did the beadwork to make a rosary.

Our next day's work involved crouching for hours at a time.
Bats made a concerted screeching noise.
We were temporarily free of domestic tasks.

6.

Tuesday we crouched for ten hours.
The foreman carried a willow switch.
At lunch we talked about the possibility of wives.
Alan said that church was the fastest route to a wife.
He looked at me and said, "We are inland people.
We conduct glory."
We mimed bad words with our legs.
Gratitude terrified us.
The foreman said, "Dream of me tonight, at the top of the stairs."
After work we were to be given temporary housing in the ruins of an abandoned
                                                        paint factory.
In my orange shirt I was like a lily.

We rode inside a moving truck.
At our new home there was no electricity or telephone service.
A pre-occupation officer repeated long passages from the parole handbook.
A portable toilet was brought in.
There were no rabbits.
My room was underground.
On the wall some teenagers had spray-painted "dependence upon patterned response."

The toad is noble.
I scratched the number eleven into my door.
Toads sat unmoving in the hallways and in our rooms.
Alan and Gerry and a man named Mario lived in my section.
Our walls were made from plywood sheets.
The degradation from rays of light barely reached us.
Our hands grasped all night; we were nervous riders.

The toads burrowed.

Night fell on our pettiness.

The smell of chemicals never lifted, as if the nitrogen cycle had been interrupted.

At some time in the night I felt animal movement on my left ankle.

I tried to think of the life of a woman to gain insight, but my thoughts turned
to medicine.

In the marsh thirsty animals opened themselves.

My crime was "aggravated loan default."

The crickets chirped bravely, despite the toads.

The need to mate.

I had a cramp in my buttock.

It was painful.

There were no rabbits.

In the morning a man came to wake us up.

He beat on the doors of the empty vats with a pipe until we were all awake.

It was Frank.

7.

I wanted coffee.
Something squeezed me three times a night.
Gentle care distracts us from discipline.
In autumn we will move slowly westward.
A sound got covered with flesh.
I touched a shell casing.
Gorillas can make art.
I had never been to a formal dinner; I had never lived alone.
The scratches on my door had moved.
We held tight to the rim of unintelligent behavior.

Frank owned the paint factory.
He volunteered to "look after us."
His demolition fetish was well known by former derelicts.
We had to finish crouching and a bus came to take us to the fifteenth century.
We had no private walking.
It was hot, the foreman had taken the day off to be a nudist, and we had a substitute overseer.
He held the same willow switch.
We were stunned by his endless need to sacrifice us.
He whipped Gerry and Mario on the back of the neck and yelled
"Keep working!
Research will save us from a burning heart!
Can you hear this frequency?"
He aroused my basest instincts.

So many things were wrong.
Our country's missiles were inadequate.
The roads had narrowed.

People no longer spoke the proper languages.
The labors of the body had become ineffective.
It was clear we were part of the solution.
That afternoon the overseer could not reach us with his switch.
I found an unused tea bag and put it in my pocket.

Back at "the Stain" Frank told us we had a new assignment.
He had contracted with the state to rebuild the factory.
"When I saw you men at the hanging . . ."
He held his hand to his heart.
A dead bat dropped to the floor.
"I saw the private pleasure of a child's revolution.
I saw the influence of unsuccessful greater efforts.
I saw the complete secret of puberty in an inkblot."
Frank was a born leader.

Our mail service was reinstated.
It seemed important to the county that we receive the official mail.
I got a postcard from George.
It read *The force of childbirth propels me still.*
Your carcass is sweet.
Terror of the body is an endless frontier.

I taped it to my front door.
A toad crouched in each corner of my room.

8.

We no longer went to work, we were already there.
The foreman came to us in our private dreams, he occurred like a warped clock or a
                                                                         drunk with shaky hands.
We enjoyed no laundry service.
Frank woke us, foreman in tow.
They lined us up on the south end.
No traditions had developed.
We began by gutting the ruins.
Frank had a tumor in his left forearm, he told it over a megaphone.
I touched something sharp and bled most of the morning.

Large dumpsters sat on each end of the grounds.
The factory's south end was open to the elements.
I felt an unmapped rustling, I was working from home.
I found a dead cow next to the outside wall.
The foreman rounded up six of us to drag it to the dumpster.
When we grabbed at the legs, the cow's stomach churned as if it were still alive.
We stepped back and the foreman poked around with a piece of lumber.
Two large possum ran from a hole beneath the cow's hind leg.
Mario vomited, the foreman docked him half an hour.

We went shirtless at work and saved our orange shirts for town.
Frank worked us for twelve hours.
The static gases relented.
We called our home the Stain, but with affection.
Gerry apologized into space.
He wanted to live now.
He made positive slogans: *Individuals are more dependable than radios.*

We ate lunch outside.

Frank and the foreman watched us through a telescope.

They had reinforced the wooden tower.

It seemed we had delivered ourselves in the underground cells.

A line of geese crossed the sky.

We knew restaurants existed.

That banks had mechanical eyes.

The ribs of the cow became important.

The foreman told us to quit working and go back to our rooms.

Frank held the megaphone to his mouth: *The grease of dead
    beggars will not go in vain.* We had promise.

9.

That night Frank gave us the talking cure.
There existed one crying shred of sky.
We each ate the small white pill.
We discovered codes.
We built a fire and attracted moths, which attracted bats.
We stood and talked ourselves smooth.

I was conscious of the rivets in my pants.
Our voyage shifted desires; we were the sons of basic science.
I told Gerry about my crime.
It was illegal for us to claim that we were innocent once we had been found guilty.
In the firelight I saw queens, graves, wings, houses, wheels, teeth.
We found a fascinating refrigerator door.
We lit cigarettes with an extravagant hand. I felt like a tusk growing from an
old elephant.

In the morning I awoke to Frank's megaphone:
It is good business to take money from cruel people.
The police also have nipples.
These are public sounds.
He was becoming a revolutionary.
His potbelly shook.
The foreman brought leftover baked goods and did not like the situation.
I came away into wildness.
I felt an irregular area in my mouth.
We were given shovels.
The foreman whipped Mario's leg with a dull piece of barbed wire.
I dug a hole next to the outside wall.

Two men waited behind me to sink a beam.
Behind that, two men mixed concrete by hand.

At that moment a church wind reached Frank.
I was given the name Helen.
The foreman turned to me.
A blackbird screamed.
Frank knelt to pray.
Each of us had a bare thought that suckled the fields.
I felt the barb whip into my calf and stick there.
The foreman yanked at it.
The flesh pulled and then gave.
I was a flight path.
I dug for the virgins who made the lace.
I dug for the birth of chrome.
I dug the number eleven into our warders.
I made a hole that thousands of people could die in.
The foreman brought the wire down.
Frank said, "Amen."
I made a mocking gesture with the curve of my tongue.

There was no lunch.
We were born by turning the edge of water; we were protected by a god
                                                                    with blue hands.
The foreman could sense our freedom.
It felt better to be punished than educated.
Our people had covered us with testimony and we turned our heads away.
I dug holes and dragged sandbags.
For inspiration, Frank read aloud the procedure for dissecting a mosquito.
The foreman missed no one.

10.

That night as I slept I saw the rope.

It was coarse and an inch thick.

I saw the hangman prepare the rope and felt what his hands felt.

This hanging was exactly the same, though it happened in daylight.

The priest walked into the prison yard.

He held a crucifix in his right hand.

Two men stood on the scaffold waiting, shifting from side to side.

Pigeons crossed over, there was nowhere for them to land.

Guards led a slouched figure through the chain-link gate.

Heads turned.

Several people clasped their hands in prayer.

Random shouts arose.

I heard the heaviness of the guards on the hollow stairs.

A cloud blocked the sun and people stopped squinting.

One of the nervous men stepped forward and held the rope still.

A dog barked.

Everyone fantasizes of open combat.

>The workers will begin a period of disruption and bloody struggle:
>the hunger of the pelvic animal, the snoring of untamed water
>against a rock beach, the desert's offer to turn us back to light.

I pulled weeds and made little furniture.

I deposited seventeen miniaturized ovens into the era before 1949.

I borrowed pitchforks from the village children.

But still the hangman kept coming.

Odors disappeared.

The priest read from his book.

The crowd stopped jostling and the prisoner stepped forward.

Some little bodies were not even born yet.

Rain fell onto a bed.

The prisoner stretched his throat.

He watched another pigeon crossing over.

Some pickles got made in a bathtub.

Action continually; yeast, farmers, and acid.

The silence before the trap opened.

A man with a raised hand stood behind the prisoner, like a shadow.

Everyone watched him.

Then his hand dropped.

11.

Wednesday evening I attended a religious class.
I had studied the techniques of sex by watching animals.
I wanted the placid years of marriage to unfold.
I had purchased a handmade wallet.
The priest said that orange shirts were welcome.
That repentance was like a slender canoe.
Recently several drummers had died during an eclipse.
These were evil days.
I turned to a large woman next to me and said,
"I am looking for a suitable wife.
Do the widows need comfort?"
The priest frowned and read from a "little-known" text:

> *Let yourself rage toward the appointed hour,*
> *like the sea rushing away toward the divine stranger's house*
> *on our day of thirst.*
> *The seven claws, the wooden mouths,*
> *the beatific statements of the horizon are signs*
> *to help us remember that day.*
> *Put down your paper memories in a basket of wine*
> *and let the blood shrink your fears.*
> *Amen.*

He was making it up.
His mouth and fingers shook.
The large woman put her hand on my hand.
Outside a squirrel circled the trunk of a tree.
"I do not curse or strike at people," I said.
"I have upward mobility."

The priest cleared his throat.

He took me into the hall.

"In the service of God," he said, "I'll roundhouse you."

I fled.

Mill Park was deserted, the statue continued its erosion.

I walked back to the Stain.

As I got closer, I saw them standing by the fire again.

The talking cure.

I asked for a pill but there were none left.

At my door I found a postcard from George.

I sat on my plywood bed.

The postcard showed a bull and a matador.

On the back he had written

> *A gunmetal lover relates his triumph.*
> *I have converted a clamshell full of blood into spontaneous fire.*
> *You must remember our nights on the Riviera, the stagnant waters,*
> *the disappearance of our machine.*
> *Your sins are flagrant.*

At that moment Gerry came into my room.

He said, "I was born beside a strip mine.

Do you know if an ostrich has hooves?

I have seen you, sleeping.

Without fear.

I was born next to a saloon . . ."

His eyes jerked.

I led him out the door.

There were forty or fifty toads in the hall.

"Stop talking" I said, and I kissed him.

He walked back to the fire.

12.

We were to work through the weekend, with promises of great reward.
We had no method for measuring angles.
The Stain had taken on a cubist quality.
The foreman grew ceremonious.
Several of us were designated "unclean."
Mario's leg had begun to fester.
He was told to find a witch bound to a gorilla, a cow untied at marriage, the effigy of
a saint dipped in kerosene.
The toads had thinned.
It was illegal for us to enter the spirit world.

We worked by light of dawn.
Frank pulled the foreman aside.
They walked in circles.
The fire still smoked.
I had the desire to ransack an apron.
I worked on the new roof with Gerry.
A dozen crows flew by without making sound.
I could see the park and the square of storefronts surrounding it.
I could see that each cloud was perfect.
We heard a small popping sound behind the Stain.
There was a dull serpent embedded in the land.
Gerry worked the pulley for a new bucket of hot tar.
We had special terms for neglect.

At lunch the foreman wore a bandage over his leg.
Blood seeped through it.
I had not jumped off any roof.

Our frothy sweat developed a language.
We seemed to be replacing the toads.
We ate tortillas and olives.
Rumor spread that Frank had shot the foreman.
Yet they seemed amicable.
Vultures circled a mile to the west.
A squirrel approached the table.
All the wishes of the world seemed audible.
I wanted a wife. I wanted to become as an animal.
The work would never end.
The conditions of parole were always temporary.
It was hard to think.

13.

We made extravagant promises to Frank.
We would expand our vocabularies.
We would finish the shell of the building in a week.
He made extravagant promises in return.
He assured us food, wives, the services of the church.
He wore a holster.
Clouds came and stayed.
We liked the hardware we held.
Our fathers ran in place, wagons passed.
In my dreams I met no one.

Gerry had received the evil eye.
I tried to find a live duck to rub on his body.
I tried to find the person and request a sweaty T-shirt to boil a soup from.
The days became unbearable.
Nights were either unbearable or there was the cure.
We had too much freedom.
We began to impose our own rules on top of the county's.
No secret cabinets.
No details of the sexual parts of unknown bodies.
No taming of animals, including toads.
No shared possessions.

One night as I slept, my hands opened a rabbit.
I unwrapped a thousand angels and everything was warm.
I built a fire and mounted it.
Noise looked like mirrors.
All the buses and trains put their shadows in my stomach.
There were clean and wonderful bandages to fondle.

The foreman woke us each with a volley of obscene whispers.
I ate crumbs from a box of croutons.
Our work resembled the movements of birds.
It was payday.
At lunch Frank's wife brought a metal lockbox full of cash.
No one received the same amount.
The figures seemed random.
I noticed that Mario's hair had begun to grow long and he was unshaven.
His wound was wrapped in a shred of orange cloth.
He was unclean and we had naturally begun to shun him.

By evening the roof was waterproof.
There were frames where interior walls would be.
Our laundry service had been reinstated.
A clean orange shirt sat on my bed.
Beneath it a postcard:

> *Some teeth on the wall and a long cord on the floor.*
> *A half-eaten pan of brownies.*
> *It is careless to stare.*
> *Some perishables traded for a profit.*
> *Prepare your tobacco for the ceremony of death, my sweet other.*

14.

That evening I walked to the Roadhouse High Club.
I walked like an inheritor.
Darkness came and answered questions.
My money was folded three times.
I did not want to flounder in public.
I walked through a museum that distinguished hardship from prosperity.
Lawn ornaments gradually lost their color.

The doorman said, "We have a tendency to be used in transactions."
I took my place at a small half booth.
There was no one to cook.
A woman placed a bubbling glass of beer in front of me.
The band played *Falling at the Door*.
As a people, we listened.
We drank the things that others would not drink.
We provided a steady supply of court cases.
Two men danced.
A minute hand moved.
A rooster crowed from behind the building.
My orange shirt, so clean.
I had never seen a kangaroo's jaw close-up.

Three women sat at a small round table.
The foreman walked in, displaying an enormous dim feeling.
A globe spun.
I said to one of the women, "Developments demand a dance."
She said, "Go ahead, evolve."
The third woman, and always the prize of being haunted.

Dark leaves moved through an open cemetery.
Elderly men synchronized the stars.
Her face was damaged.
She allowed me a sip from her beer.

Some animals are given the names of their cries.
Birds may have fatal habits.
Any leopard vibrates at a frequency a good deer can hear.
When it is time to mate, the cockroach speaks in the voice of Old Glory.
Little is known.
In fluency of embrace the alligator has advantages.
During mating season, the emperor spider withholds its vocabulary of strin
Baboons spit pulp as a form of gratitude.

"I live in room 11." I said.
 She would not look at me, which I took as encouragement.
 I knew that if I did not work I would return to jail.
 If I returned to jail I would not have to work.
"Could we dance?
 Could we have malaria together?
 Could we study karate?"
 Some torn clapping.
 Slumping in the crowded room.
 The waitress pretended to play the fiddle.
 I said, "We can dance tomorrow," and finished my beer.
 On the walk home, I had opinions.

15.

The ghost note sounded.

The hands took deep, gentle breaths in the suburbs, on a donkey.

Mario began to die.

I was embarrassed.

I had a spiritual bias against clipped hedges.

Monkeys were bad news to an opium field.

When I woke up the foreman sat moaning in the corner.

He was small.

The rumpled hours.

I woke up again.

Someone said, "Animals and soldiers get little mail.

Seventy percent of our love is the quality of the accusations."

It was time for work.

Gerry and I carried sheetrock.

It brought coolness against the length of my arm.

We were not in hyena country.

He said, "Don't you want to know my crime?"

He used his skin for shelter.

The sounds that Frank made into the megaphone grew theatrical and futile.

I had a lithe streak.

I had a streak of crackling passion.

Frank said, "A dead man is giving orders."

A building contains too much.

It is hard to dream in a bright room.

Our rebellion had liberated the boundaries of hysteria.

The shapes of our heads were sometimes determined by alcoholism.

The foreman loved paper money.
His voice touched our new window frames and we grew resentful.
Some on the crew were threatened by a good meal.
The fenceposts were engineered for group effort.
A shovel stuck upright from a deep hole.

We were the men who "lived at that dreadful place."
We built a stone woman in a nearby cemetery, out of the names of people.
We built a cold inner history.
We constructed a device for public attack.
We controlled the damages of yesterday, no extra charge.
We were yellow public rubbish at dawn, building answers too long to be expected
This wreckage of shrunken faces, words diminish it.

I waited on the number seven bench.
The foreman read my name.
I have been docked two hours for cursing.
I imagined him wearing an apron.
Or being eaten by a ghost dog.
I imagined planting my shovel into him.
I thought *When we go to church I will stand back from the priest.*
I will ask why we never see ghosts french kissing.
We see them standing by the side of the road, never blinking, holding back a dog that
comes at the crack of dusk to eat
I said the word "shovel" until it sounded like a beautiful comet hitting the
foreman's mind.

Gerry had become sentimental.
A sparrow had died.
He said, "My crime was counterfeiting.
We all do that."

He was crying.

The sun was undeniably proficient.

Mario had stopped working.

He stood in a corner disguised as a pet feeling.

We were not permitted to drink for profit.

We happened to know everything.

Maneuvers of power were banned at night.

Gerry wept.

I felt like a searchlight trained on a mouse.

16.

Rumor spread that the parole board had adopted slightly older personalities.
Gerry's glow seemed in constant wobble.
By evening pigmentation from dust obscured our names.
Mario followed the same white bird down traffic.
Rumor also of veterans weeding tomatoes.
Everything was workaday.
We slept with our money.
I played lost in a glimmering smell.
The liberation of the masses looked delicious, an ornament for being pretty.

Work ended when the foreman made a sinister dog voice.
I found so many places for my pillow.
Mario's mouth blackened.
As I starved I saw one small gray eye.
Each night it was either the talking cure or Roadhouse High Club or sleep.
Gerry had become religious since the evil eye.
He made decisions without interest.

Mario walked to the roof.
There must have been clouds.
There must have been suckerfish in rivers.
A sound perhaps had been arranged.
Mario sat low and stabbed hard.
He changed like the end of a whip.
A small shadow became large.
A long hour pressed the onlookers.
I opened myself to the efforts of each creature.
Mario ceased his spasms.

Four of us surrounded him.
Each took hold of a limb.
An animal forgave Mario.
We heaved him from the roof.

A mind must be used to think.
The horizon was a wisp.
I started walking.
Mario swelled in the dirt.
His parole was over.
I tried to remember the words that stopped me.
Coal and salt in the earth held their value.
A nurse or a teacher or a mayor all drank heavily after curfew.
Thin civilians read mystery stories.
The streets of any town are a product of the mind.
In prison a funeral was treated as theater.
A light went out as I approached.
I saw a train full of cheap cooking.
I walked without Mario's cheer.
In the roadhouse nobody was dead.
An airplane flew over the parking lot.
Messages of punishment were slowly coming to an end.

17.

A song with unknown effects waited behind the roadhouse door.
What matters most is what is impossible.
The doorman said, "Human appetite is voluntary.
Tonight's special includes ordinary flesh and bones.
Please keep to the right."
I found a table.
It was engraved with a likeness of deer.
The waitress brought the customary drink.
Energy comes from the curvature of the leg.
My history was reduced to an act of the eye.
On the contrary.

The woman's face was still hidden.
I opened my lips and began talking, "I worked several days in a watertight enclosure
to get here.

Are you available for this?
I am doing the weakest job.
But some people just sip tea."
She spoke but I did not hear it.
I could only afford one drink.
Even a garden plot has a schedule.
I leaned close to her.
It was dark.
"You should witness the great tenderness of the worker's day off," I said.
She nodded.
Hands flew up.
The song was called "Outside the Party."
People danced in a line.

A disturbance of chairs ensued.

Two orange shirts were on the ground.

When friends arrive in church wearing bullets!

We left by the side door, especially.

It was dark.

I asked to walk her home.

She seemed to continue nodding.

She said, "Some prisoners specialize in shriveling a golf ball with their minds.

In silent miles we are the almost fifty melancholy sounds attributed to

    Frederick Douglass. Echoes become further damaged or are corrected.

Yourself excluded."

I held her hand.

A car veered.

The progress we made fell blandly into place.

18.

The foreman had an elbow for my dreams.
A great invasion of hands.
We were doing the monstrous, degenerate work of waiting.
You learn to expect lies, even in a drop of rain.
The building was close to finished but we didn't know how to finish.
I saw the empty pattern of another world.
My orange shirt lied to me.
I was close to being a different worker.

Someone had some weeping business and the foreman retaliated.
When I became faint I smelled a bottle of burnt hair.
We could drill directly into concrete, sink a bolt, steady an awning.
Some lies settled in the kingdom of our hands and made the word for "knife."
I watched Frank speak like too much pepper falling from a shaker.
There came a cold morning light. I knew our factory would never run.
The factory was built for manufacturing us.

It was decided to put in a retaining wall by the loading dock, ten feet from Marie
point of impa
Frank said into his megaphone *Charlie Chaplin sat on a pin, how many inches
did it go in?*
The streets wanted to become solemn.
Birds were building a nest.
I ran a string level along the earth, to see if it met our specifications.

Then Gerry turned to Frank and began screaming, "You're a pony not a judge!
You're a pony not a judge!"
Colors flew everywhere.

We were related to colors.
The foreman turned away.
The birds stopped.
Frank said, "Oh, pumpkin, can't you help me?"
We wanted Frank to sing.
Gerry said, "We sang her to sleep, let's sing her awake.
This is bad for my nerves."
The foreman urinated on the building, just round the corner.
Frank calmed us with his megaphone.
Morale was declining.

A snake can learn routines.
It can begin to know the mailman.
A lizard may have a guilty face.
In the case of history, small flocks of birds have suddenly changed the dominant culture.
A young animal, such as a calf, must be kept safely away from drugs, government,
                                                  and the underworld.
The earth was not level, it was curved.
We made the explanation to the foreman, who spat.
We built the wall from blocks; there came no awkward pauses.
At the end of the day bells aligned their rings and began to spread.
A breeze came along.
I didn't want to act as mean as a human being.
The foreman gave us flea powder and sent us to bed.

19.

Next morning Frank was narrow.

I saw mockingbirds changing trees.

A cup and saucer were broken by the wind.

The foreman's body was laid out on the loading dock like a large dinner fish.

We awoke late, afraid of our flimsy hearts.

Frank called for an assembly, megaphone set on proud.

A coyote would have in its small head a sound for life and a sound for death.

Gerry poked the foreman with a tentative finger then made an awkward cross.

A squirrel flicked its tail.

"I shot him," Frank said sadly.

We suddenly began relaxing.

The foreman was dead.

I thought of swimming.

From the edge of town we heard a marching band.

High school tuba and funny socks.

"It isn't fair to talk," Frank said.

He pointed to a stack of shovels.

The foreman had bullet holes in his back.

It looked like a golf course there.

It was nothing new to be guilty.

I noticed a constellation of nests.

Four men had been kissed by a dream and began digging the grave.

Some of us believe the act of theft is symbolic of the sex act.

A body ends with a blotting motion; a little shack of tidal movements that
    has ceased. "Do not strike water," Frank commanded.

He wore a bonnet and the megaphone hung from his right hand.

We lifted the foreman into pastoral details.
His sack landed in the hole.
Frank visited with someone's empty boots.
We covered the big calm stomach with dirt.
It was like burying a chess piece.
Lunch would be smooth, exploring the inner regions of a motorcycle through the
mind of a fish.

Some of us believed in shrinking into nothingness.
We went to classes for it.
The foreman's tongue lay dead in his mouth.
We were visited by a sleepwalker's moon.

Each of us was given a rake to make ourselves pure.
I exerted my pressure onto Earth.
Our business kept changing, we envisioned kissing as the middle-class act.
At the end of my shift I found a postcard on my bed.
It showed some unusually large innards on a butcher's table.
The back read:

> *I have a garden that my left hand reached into.*
> *I will kill the sweet talk you whispered to your father.*
> *It won't hurt to grow smaller.*
> *Think of the scars a ghost must have.*

The foreman was dead.
In the hallway Frank said, "I spit colors" and wandered off.

20.

I ran through a barrier of milk.
The foreman blushed and owned dogs.
I ate false caviar in a time capsule and waited, while the marching band improved
along the beach.
Morning grew its edge.
I woke clutching the postcard, naked throat, blue fingers feeding myself to myself.

The foreman remained dead.
I was aware of his tongue shriveling under the earth.
Another breeze passed through our rooms, the second one.
I heard a truck grinding backwards outside and prepared to be taken.
Dawn dropped a rush of stars along the floor.
George had not killed me yet.
Frank entered the hallway with a dog.
He said, "Boys, meet the new foreman."
A nervous-necked dog.
The parole board would not like it.
The woman from the bar would not like it.
I leapt forward and found my orange shirt.

The windows and insulation had arrived.
The dead foreman became weather.
We emptied the truck and smelled an old rain, from the forties.
Thousands of grasshoppers were having sex.
I could not ask the new foreman dog for gloves.
Gerry became a silhouette, swollen at the back of a play.

Our work made the government's hands brighter.
Some animals' days are filled with song.
We didn't know the thrill of our factory's barbed-wire fences.
The foreman dog had no chance to have a real face.
I saw fifty blue versions of paradise in the sky.
When the truck was gone I felt dislodged from the present, a bubble rising
    from grass. The new foreman whined.
Insulation made each breath an almost final art form.
I worked a staple gun until the foreman barked us home.

Frank said things would change soon.
He stood in the center of the factory and gave our last talking cure.
The pill cracked me from the nucleus out, famous for six minutes.
I heard the fire outside speaking to a foreign operator.
Mario's blood wailed in our throats.
I had a need to visit the deeply drawn fizz of the fields.
The woman was still nodding to me, she slept in a bed.
I wore my surprised face in a corner with Gerry and Alan.
Gerry said, "He can track you, the new foreman.
He can look at you and make you old.
I'm scraping for a disappearance."
I said, "Gerry, we have to be willing to listen to the mules.
To the squeak of the downtown booths.
To the stains on the old tourists."
A crow flew down near the fire.
It liked home cooking, I could tell.

21.

The next two nights I went to Roadhouse High Club, but the woman kept away.
Meanwhile smoke fell.
Meanwhile passed in an oscillating trickle.
A mattress echo found its way down the street.
She had a weakness for vanishing, like the buffalo.
One night the band caused us pain, singing in their robes.
Next night the silence in a shoebox had reached under the barstool for a body.
I walked late and watched for animal eyes.
I had liberated myself from economics by nodding along.
My pockets made my hands giddy.

Someone appeared at my elbow, near the street corner.
I heard the sound of paper folding.
It was the foreman dog.
I heard the sound of ice cubes in a glass.
I heard the dog whine and I had that hopeless smile of someone's listening
to the radio.
The foreman dog walked me back to the factory.
The hair on my legs touched my trousers and made me feel weak.

At the railroad bridge I urinated against the concrete while he watched with a certa
motherly affection.
Handles shone.
The skeleton protects specific rooms of the body.
The high road was gentle.
Bats worked the air's moving holes.

Rain entered the courtyard like a bellboy.
I saw the foreman sit up from the earth, wearing a cocktail dress.
A parrot unfolded its shore-beaten language.
I asked it to say the words for "blue."
Each day to dream and wake is too much business out of nothing.
I heard the foreman dog's nails click in the hall.

When an animal charges, it is usually a last resort.
I saw far-off touching in tiny backseats.
The door opened and I felt the cold wet nose.
The men at the hanging must have made a sound from dreams.
I examined fruit grown from the mouths of spiders.
To live simply, as a ship landing.
I found myself in the hallway, following the others.
Gerry recited his morning prayer as we walked, and I nodded to the satellites that
                              moved through the nearest reaches of space.
Squirrels know how the buried thing changes and is reborn.
I watched them in the trees as I put on my gloves.

22.

By the end of the week the building was finished.
Each of us privately felt that we had built ourselves.
Gerry pressed buttons and tightened screws.
There was no proper electricity.
We were waiting for those electric men and their fifty or more tricks.
I felt that the foreman dog watched me especially.

In our county trees were yellowing.
The frogs sobbed.
Everything looked tiny, as on Jupiter.
It was a violation of parole to walk backwards on the job.
I gave a speech then, because even hair lived once.
And I saw girls.

Monday was to be for clean-up.
When I walked out the front gate on Friday, the mist had disappeared unde
                                        the counterattack.
Chanting and swaying.
Horns grew.
Camels stumbled.
The woman stood on the high road, waiting.

She said, "I have seen ghosts on the roads, riding in buses.
Transient thoughts of browned-out cities.
Riding in the backs of pick-up trucks, ghost hair whipping into their eyes.
Ghost dogs jumping from bridges.
I live in another world where I am your foreman's master."

I yellowed.

An easy color scraped from the bottom of a bathtub.

She said, "I walk the way a sailor walks. The ghost world is just beneath the blade
        of your shovel, you hear it hit something, not quite metal, the bones of
        something lost, you call the foreman over—look at this—someone's pet
        buried behind the factory, the little jawbone, a small foreleg you could snap
        and look inside."

She nodded the entire time.

I felt a turning in me as a light turns above an ambulance.

She continued, "Once people believed there was a bone for the soul, everything else
                                                        rotted away.

I've seen a dog in the ghost place at the top of my ceiling, where I am the master.

Your foreman waits at the end of a chain for me to pull.

At six o'clock when the cracks of dusk just open I see ghosts walking the road with us.

They wear orange shirts and open cupboard doors and look for the flesh."

We walked to the church.

A few seconds of drying cement.

The priest worried like an engine for hours, his sullen mouth trembling and blank.

We waited at a red line painted on the hallway, ten feet from his office.

You can be fined for crowding a priest.

23.

Some animals have so little.
Small pigs buzz and sing.
A macaw plays with orange and gives grace.
A snail understands the presence of autumn evenings.

"Are you crossing inside?" the priest asked us.
I said, "I've got the laundry arm from the old radio factory."
The priest squinted.
A bird began to run and laugh.
The woman was named Mel that day.
The priest stood.
He shook.
He took children down from the sky.
We let the wind blow.
His hands found a basin of dirt and he threw a handful on each of us.
The caterpillars were dead or had become moths.

"What are *love manners*?" he asked us.
We did not know and he bled us for half an hour, into bowls.
It hurt like a dream hurts.
Aural luminosity waned.
"Why do you wish to be married?" he asked.

She answered, "Because of some dusty road in an August thundershower."

"Religion," he began, "streamlines the object.
As you hump in bed you will have uniform energy loss.
The observer will appear to travel faster than sound.

The observer will be me.
There is a god for every ripple present on a liquid's surface.
Your souls are exactly one hundred meters deep."

He wept a little.
Outside, the pay telephones filled with moss.

He crossed himself and resumed.
"In the larger rooms of heaven, gods are placed one hundred meters apart.
What is the role played by raindrops in the flow of god's current?
Well you are not scientists.
Your dreams must ignore surfaces of any kind."
Mel stood and grabbed his wrist.
A cloud tried to get into the room.
The priest signed a form and passed it across his desk to us.
I wanted to be near the foreman dog.
The priest said, "A judge can react to this."

We heard a knock at the door.
Someone had violated the red line.
At that moment we became engaged.
A bird began to be normal.
We were all nodding.

24.

Monday morning the foreman dog lunged.

Frank began the day like the dull edge of a comic book.

Gerry was changing his bandages in the hallway.

He handed me a postcard.

It read *O.K., phone-face.*

> *Point of order.*
> *Imagine the devil, full force inside an egg.*
> *Can you hear my hands jerking us forward in a deserted bakery?*
> *Love's sweet sorrow dying in tights like a strip of steam.*
> *I will give you one day in my army.*

Frank lined us up.

The foreman dog paced.

Every surface at the Stain had been touched by a convict's hands.

Bird sounds lived inside wind sounds.

I thought of a tennis court and my thought went unanswered.

Bats clutched in sleep.

The wings of nowhere filled up; the old days formed thin crosses.

We waited.

Frank's wife appeared.

She demonstrated impatience.

Frank gave his speech.

"Make everything stop.

Think of blood spoiling underground and old people who fill up with smoke.

I don't know something and it isn't among the stars."

Frank's wife shifted her weight repeatedly.

"It is in the movement apart of things from each other.

Like you men.
Rate of travel."
Far away a whistle blew.
Twice.
Three times.
"This is Mary."
Frank pointed to his wife with his thumb.
Four times the whistle.
Five.
The foreman dog held his head at an angle.
Frank asked us to get down on our knees.

Frank's wife finally spoke.
She looked like a hollow tree with a handsome face that squirrels could crawl
                                                    in and out of.
She said, "Erosion is not symmetrical, no, your life, you see, crosses, it crosses past
        recorded time, and you are totally free, but only in that sense, and yes, as in
        part of the constant total mass, you are free, but must go back now.
To the program.
Get your things."

The whistle started up again.
A voice carried in from the road.
There were magnets in the clocks.
The insides of our bodies all slick.
We stood up.
The foreman dog made a small bark without opening his mouth.
"We'll have a little show," Frank said.
"A form of prayer."
The whistle blew.
A blackbird walked on the earth.

Mary and Frank turned and moved toward the gate.

Gerry's bandages were loose and they flapped in the wind.

I wondered what she meant by "things."

25.

It was against the rules to profit from the pre-occupational program.
I gathered my extra set of clothing and my postcards.
Gerry held a page from a magazine.
Excessive personal effects were forbidden.
Alan carried two toads, one in each palm.
It was against our code.

The "electricians" had been bringing in wires all morning.
We had taken so many breaths of our neighborhood sky.
Frank lined us up and counted.
We waited behind the fence, along the road, staring in.
Three men wearing hard hats walked toward us.
Frank held his megaphone.
The foreman shat.

I had the feeling that rows of crops were going unharvested.
That hens looked into the earth and saw a puzzle.
The three men joined Frank and Mary.
We all waited by the fence.
Several newspapers continued to wrinkle in the ditch.
Frank turned to us and spoke through the megaphone, "Change must be made.
Without losing rhythm. You men have excited the public imagination.
Thank you."

There were no birds or rabbits or turtles or earthworms or beetles or squirrels
                                                                        moving.
Frank turned to the three men and said, "Let it go."

Sound one.

The battlefields of commerce.

Then sound two.

The building became mostly smoke, falling and falling with nowhere to go.

Frank was jumping off the ground.

The men in hard hats took pictures.

A short, pale convict we knew only as "Bucket" made a run for it.

The foreman dog dragged him down by his orange shirt, ripping from side to side

The building collapsed and echoed.

The dog bit into Bucket, took skin from his back. Pieces fell.

Mary shifted her weight. Gerry cried.

A rabbit crossed the grounds, unsure and jumping.

I held tight to the fence with one hand.

My personal effects in the other.

Some animals organize to save grain for food.

Frank had destroyed us so slowly we never noticed.

Some animals seem to forget their children.

The air was naked and bright where the building had stood.

Frank's demolition of the Stain was nothing, an afterthought.

There came a pressure from all directions.

Frank said, "Onward."

As I walked I watched the ground for signs.

I saw a discarded toad.

Broken glass.

Scrap of paper.

We were given sticks to beat together, to warn others of our approach.

26.

They moved us to a temporary detention center on the fairgrounds.
It was against the rules to wander aimlessly, hands at our sides.
We could not have lingering doubts.
Horror was forbidden.
We scraped paint from the grandstand for hours, a dozen little insect noises from
                                                    the ends of our blades.
There was no defense from sound.

I received two items atop my cot.
The first was a postcard from George.
I thought how the earth gives free rides in a circle.
I didn't read the card.
The second mailing was sent to indicate a parole meeting.
Outside a lumpy raven squawked.
I saw the patterns of trash that made us touch ourselves at lunch.
Gerry said, "You will probably be free to sign receipts and read books soon."
He stood near his cot and crossed himself.

The woman had agreed to attend my parole meeting.
She controlled the papers from the priest.
We knew that airplanes tempted us to do wrong.
That disappointment could stop the growth of leaves on branches.
Still, one has the right to do something.

I walked to the statue at Mill Park.
It was night.
A woman curried a horse.
A policeman gave directions to a truck driver.
My orange shirt.

I felt a flowing, as of water or air.
I saw the woman's nodding head.

We arranged.
Crickets moved in and then out.
The whole smile is found in every genus, if not species.
We only nodded together.
And arranged.
The horse was well curried.
Upon leaving we swam for a moment, across the floor of the town.
As I approached the grounds, I watched for the foreman dog.

We slept in one big room at the fairgrounds.
The building displayed a sign over its entrance stating, "*small animal exhibit.*"
The postcard was still on my cot.
It showed protozoa in Lone Ranger masks.
The back read:

> *We can starve like empty ropes.*
> *Children are learning to weave the fat of pigs.*
> *Does your mouth go strange at a pillow's meow?*
> *I am driven male by the thought of police wandering in sports jackets.*
> *Other men are just wallpaper with fists.*

I practiced signing my name, and dreamt.
The fairgrounds held residual acts, in and out of water.
My cot creaked.
Gerry knelt beside me.
"I have been called," he said.
"I want to be used in a cake.
I rented a ladder by telephone . . ."
He drifted into sleep.
I could hear something far off, ropes dangling, a pony munching grass, someo
alphabetizing the items in a room.

27

The courthouse was wet and we knew it.
I had gotten lost in the bathroom, so many doors.
An officer of the court held up one finger.
I assumed the position of a ripe strawberry.
Oh lovely.
Another officer led Frank into the courtroom.
He gestured at me and said, "I can vouch for that one.
He believes."
Frank's handcuffs gleamed.
We are stars we are stars.

I was called.
A sparrow crossed the room, the transom gaping open.
I saw the woman in the back row, nodding.
A single animal sound can last as long as eight years.
Then there is the sound of Earth turning.
An officer of the court said, "Pre-occupational."
The judge looked at paper.
The woman nodded.
Frank stared straight ahead, a cheap gadget.

"There are places," the judge began, "in the unprobed mind.
Places where we moan to lose.
I am meant to deliver you from those places."
The sparrow fluffed.
A grasshopper crossed its legs.
I thought I heard a hurdy-gurdy machine.

"I will ask you five questions."
The judge read slowly from a note card.
"Do you understand this language?
Can you work?
Will you be faithful in your marriage?
Are we altered by the medium through which we travel?
Do you have bus fare?"

My star climbed its hill.
Again I mounted and again I tried.
I nodded my head.
The bathrooms were haunted.
The woman nodded.
Pages leaned in and to the left.
My willful answers held the scent of pony grass.
I nodded and nodded.
There came no scraping sounds.

"Regular processes often produce random results."
The judge handed the officer a piece of paper with my new
    address on it.
"You are on restricted parole."
Frank began crying.

At the fairgrounds word spread.
It was my last night.
"We are death's vehicle," Gerry said, then stopped talking.
I was shunned.
My cot didn't mean anything.
The lull of small sleeping animals.
Puddles getting fat from heaven.

I heard evidence of demons staging desires.
It was against the rules.

In the morning I waited again.
I realized we had moved through the county like a clock.
I grew terrified of returning the day to its start.
The men walked off, each holding a scraper.

28.

A short green bus came for me.
Movement made a crow die.
The driver's bloodshot touch on the wheel, the suddenly
    stepped-on feeling, the sound of the statue's face.
We passed through the center of a field of weakness.
The fairgrounds receded like a wave.
Through the fences down the roads to the end of the city and
    to the end.

We stopped near a steep gravel driveway to a house with a
    corrugated tin roof.
The driver saluted.
I blazed away.
Demons were cutting flesh.
A gasp shook loose from the tops of trees; I kept my hands away
    from my mouth.
I had imagined this place.

We were free in many ways but then we weren't free.
Frank, for example.
I built a scary lantern to hang in the wind, first thing.
Clouds hung near the edge of the earth.
Dead wasps still chose to see the world.
A sandstorm moved in.

In the house wet clothes were becoming dry.
Lunchpails strewn all over the place.
I found a table that folded in.
On the table sat three pieces of mail.
One a postcard.
One from a job service.
The third a housing contract.
I kept watch for the dead.

There was no woman.
There was a jar to drink water from.
When danger appears there comes a little carbon dioxide.
I was faking my profile.
The postman lived in his own house, far away.
Quietly, my pants became cold.

The postcard showed a knotty pine motel swarmed by locusts.
The back read:

> *Here is the way to blow in the box.*
> *Feel the chill wheel stir?*
> *Where you live, parole is short for PARASITE.*
> *So start looking over your shoulder for a tongue in your bed.*
> *See if it has wings.*

I could feel the oceans lowering.
There rose a great force.
The end result was air, suddenly back again.

29.

They passed laws.
I slept on the softest part of the floor as the flags whipped.
I learned, in my sleep, to say good-bye.
To a heart-shaped figure who lived in my hand.
A car arrived.
Owls and rabbits started knowing about each other.
It was Frank.

I went down the hard road to see its fruits.
Frank stepped out of his sort of microscope.
Somewhere miles away from us an egg fell into promise.
"I got off-track," he said.
"I got a bruised apple."
We heard the music of saws, far and close.
"I got. I got."
He sounded exasperated.
"I'm pre-occupational.
Starting tomorrow."

I told Frank, "The air is full of bacteria.
Some of the bacteria are helpful.
I have weight and force and can blow things about."
It seemed a comfort.
The old foreman waited for us with his hooks spread.
A candle represented the sun.
I made a list of harmful things.

"I just wanted to know if you've seen my dog," Frank said.

"There's a paper world of devils and I need him."

The earth yawned.

Frank took two pills out of his pocket.

The talking cure.

I had a stiff neck for hands to go around.

Birds interrupted us and tired.

We were terrified of our ancestors, sitting on hotel beds in
 heaven.

Pill-ridden-thunder-chicken.

We did not have a fire so we stared at the house.

"I always dreamed you were my dinner," Frank started.

"When we listen to death someday, the language will be sweet
 and sour takeout.

I throw glee right out the windows.

I do.

Really the leap from whisper to forever is bobbing on the
 horizon.

How long can a person sense the grief of the universe?

By the light of the moon or in books, probably not longer.

Cha cha cha.

Hee hee."

"I can only fathom sunny scraps of you," I said.

"Your undersea life.

How your heaven freezes.

I know that.

One step ahead of you, it freezes.

I want to become small and red and disappear in a bag."

It went on through the price of oil, the slaughter of hogs, the fur coats, the lit cigarettes
the President Nixons, the rubbing of gravestones, the cutting of hair, the
suspicions, the umbrellas, the grass, the hairpin turns, the speeches in wire shoes
the clouds that lived inside us.

Then the talking stopped.

30.

At the job service a woman who was older than the earth kept changing her name.
She had drawn a circle around her desk.
People reached across it.
She wondered aloud, "What is *up* and what is *down*?"
I stayed silent as a turnstile.

A lock fell asleep and a few miracle stars rose up from the sea.

I got a new job—opening a clover to find the phenomenon of collapsing human wishes
                                                    —in the mail room.
"Be prepared to look weary," they said.
Someone got carsick in an office chair.
The lights went out.
I walked home.

At sunset, human lives murmured.
I testified to the trembling straw, even pigeons saw there was no actual woman.
There was no map-stopping groan of mountains, no waves of tulips to tell us
                                            how people die.
The world of men is a ridiculous record player.
I watched for the toads to reappear.
I almost believed in ballrooms.

The camel house swayed.
Sleep was like underlining the word "dumpling" over and over.
A voice called from beneath the sun's dark scab.
I dreamt holes right into birds, for fifteen minutes.
A truck downshifted.

The voice became religious, as a flame making a new medicine boil.
I heard noises from the holes in birds.
A call for clear direction in choosing the next age.
Where was the sandbag to place between myself and the sound of waking?
Teams of survivors shimmered in the grass.
A cabbage formed, out of sorrow.
Even it had a voice.

Eventually another moment came on.
The street, birches, hills, the air.
An ash drifted.
I waited in my bed for the first day.
Eventually, it got in my hair.

31.

It was against the conditions of parole to budget water.
I was not allowed to change trains or cough near jewelry.
In the morning I saw George at the end of the driveway.
Like a lamppost pointing to a six-foot hole made by rain.
He held a crucifix in his left hand.
"Where is your orange shirt?"

I said, "It is my turn to start sleeping and grow huge inside."
Music came as from thousands of telephones.
It was all we could hear.
It was the marching band.

The truth is there never was a woman.
She existed on paper—court document woman.
I married her, I was inside a wheel.
George seemed full of handwriting.
Rabbits reappeared.
He carried the hangman's crucifix.

"You go to work, I'm going to tie a knot."
I couldn't take another wedding.

I walked drunk and full of light until I belonged to form and color.
I saw people nodding, a door to the world of their noise.
Two rabbits turned back into darkness.

When I looked back, George was crying.
I saw a dove sleeping in its cold home.

This went on for days.

The marching band turned left and would walk forever to Roadhouse High Club.
Was Mel one pale drink of a puppet's teacup?
A side effect?
Her name stretched in the boiling hills.
Some shoppers almost embarrassed me with their soft arms.
I asked them if I was married.

At the bus stop a flicker of boredom shone.
I saw a snake forgive me.
There were the unzipped pictures of ourselves, crusted and rising.
Nothing happened, like a window inside a glass of water, and then I heard the bus,
    its gray music written by mothlight.
Each of its seats harmed the sky.
The bus driver nodded and said, "No dream sounds allowed, only syntax.
All aboard."
The lawns shone blue and silent areas were enforced.

That's when I turned to you across the aisle of the number twelve and said, "Now we
                                            live on the edge of your town
We sing the old songs.
There's a noose hanging in the living room.
We don't answer the door.
Something happened in room 11.
You should watch out."

a call, an action

prayer for dropouts

for the students of Quest Academy, 2008–09

may you not wander into the empty trailer behind the warehouse and may that
  boy's face disappear from your memory; may that boy get old and balance
  branches on his head stupidly

may those four smeary men in the clearing not notice you, may their faces distort as
  they turn to look and may they see nothing

may the reflection of the soldier in the oily water turn to salt and may the soldier
  turn to salt

may you never stay in a FEMA trailer as any waters recede, as you wait for any
  wreckage to be cleared

may the tent city disappear and may the people waiting there to hurt you
  disappear

may many versions of you carry your burden into many houses and may the
  burdens be released

may this be a prayer of correct dosage and may flowery clouds excite you

may you sit in lawn chairs drinking beer as darkness blurs the woods

may you have visions of duke ellington at the piano and may those visions fill
  with colors and what will you see in the colors? may you see nothing but the
  colors themselves

may the peacock step into your path and be still

may your red wheelbarrow fill with meteorites and transparent cities

and if there is a filing cabinet that must burn for you, may we concentrate
together until it ignites

and may your campsite turn technicolor; may clouds over the swingset never
appear apocalyptic

may you see how the ferris wheel turns like a planet for you

may your skirt fly up perfectly when you dance

may the grief-bearing flowers explode in their vases

may you lock the murky giant back in storage and later may you dance
with a tree or are those trees, perhaps they are clouds

and when the bridge is out may you cross by riding on the back of the black dog

and may there be a small silver house waiting in the clouds, a house with one
easy window through which you see you are in heaven

and when you dream may there be a fire in the center of the maze and may it warm
you, may you burn down the maze and dream again

may the textbooks fall from their shelves and rot for you, may the books
become nests and may the nests hold the birds you will become

may the abandoned submarines wash up gently for this is a red world, a dream
with many suns and when the water burns may you know the fire from its
reflection on the water, may you be discerning

may you build a garden of flowered scraps in your room and may kind people
come to the room as if to a garden

may red birds perch all across history and carry our karma though we are made
of snakes and ears and many mouths, we are swallowed by flies

may you forget the cartoon monsters chasing you down the road at twilight
because that is memory

may what grows from your body begin to green, may it not be dead or cracked
may it be just starting to live

may light hanging from the trees hypnotize you in the appropriate hour

may you walk upon the graves and know you are walking upon the graves

may you see the path through the charcoal-crusted trees

may the door to the other side not sink into the ground as it sometimes does

may the signs not go empty

and may you never be trapped in the machine worlds of the industrial park where
pipes clang and steam in blue light, not there, not in the control towers and
not on the blinding floor of the machine

instead may you see the reflections float calmly downstream, may you see the quiet
        waters of the port but never that parking lot, never the white trailer with
        no tractor

may there be an interim of explosive color against the backdrop of the void and
        may that instant be you

may singing clouds envelop your buildings

may you be immersed in the lines of color, streaked thickly with them

may the peacock's wing be made of pills and may those pills be available to you

may those two men guarding the warehouse in their thick coats keep their
        backs turned all of their cold lives

in fact may it just be a cardboard city you invented and may you look
        through little windows the size of your fingernail

and may you see all the way to a clear river

and may you tread water there until you realize you are treading light, you,
        wherever you are, alone at the booth in an empty river town,
        buying a ticket for a movie that is also your life, a movie waiting for you
        to become its field of light

and may you always watch the oak limbs paint colors in the air

and what if the meteorites in the wheelbarrow form a hat you wear to the
        vanishing point

and what if the vanishing point is a mirror

and what if we have already burned that filing cabinet tonight with our minds and
        again we see duke ellington, hands poised in your ray of light

and we see that boy try to turn into a lighthouse but we don't let him

instead we build this campsite in our dreams and it doesn't matter if they are trees
        or clouds for our lives are dreams

may you swim in the flooded christmas tree farm because it is safe, because the
        giant sits now in storage and you may twirl your skirt again to the old
        dances, freely resonant beneath the blue ribbons and flowering trees

and we have banished that active boy to a plateau

we have written nothing on the dead trees to help him, he will grow up to
        stupidly balance branches on his head

may you see the ferris wheel turn against the purple and orange sky at dusk

may a friendly buffalo come to you and know everything, may it know
        what you did in the abandoned steel mill and not care

it is a buffalo and it is not going extinct

and if you feel it's too quiet with the buffalo may there be a song

may the red birds sing for anyone trapped

and if you are inside the egg, may the birds come for you no matter how big
        the egg, even if it's a planet

and when you hatch, may you be carried across the earth by a woman, by a feather,
        by drumming

she is the woman who wove the old world, which she now balances
        casually on her head and you are free of it

and may you know how you got free

and may you receive this magic all the days of your life.

the hallucinogenists

first impression

we throw a party and the police come
they have black shoes and accessorize well
like hipsters
we immediately throw another party
the police come back
they are enchanted with our music
it calls to them
their fists love our doors
I have been in this kind of relationship before

the police leave
they drive through the night to end another party
we must think of them in the morning
how an officer sits at the edge of a mattress
afraid of a new day
fumbling with the silk edge of a blanket for comfort

the police want us to think of others
and to stop having this good time
but everything that happens is just something
we made up a moment ago

and when the police tell us not to be so happy
we ask them where they get their shoes

it is unspeakably early in our lives
we want to come to our own parties
as other people—then we'd show us how to live
we want to come to our party as the police

we want to be others
it is wrong but still we want to

some people keep a record of their most loved moments
on scraps of paper in a coffee can
we want to be something we just made up
when the song ends
we want the next song to make us happy

the police drive through the night on pursuit tires
we know where they get their shoes
we show them how to live
fumbling with the silk edge of a blanket for comfort
writing their names on scraps of paper
to put in a coffee can
we want them to come back

ode to mescaline

Cold flower walks back and forth in the shy body.
Cactus petal swims in the hungry body.
Green vapor sings in the fever body.
The stomach goes away down a hard road.
Here comes a fireworks body.
Father flies through clouds.
Mother rises through earth.
I admire each leaf.
The sky pleases each day.
We'll give our hair back to earth.
Even the armpit, even the ditch has a pleasing fashion.
What if I were a mango?
Smell how the grass loves us.
Feel the tongue of the cloud.
A listener praises the sound of fire.
See our shadows have dignity.
Our headaches have their own lives, like moons.
I set aside a day for clouds, a night for clouds.
It grows green light inside me.
There is nothing to resist.
Sometimes I am nothing.
The tongue of the cloud cleans each word.
The sweet offering of the voice makes a way.
Any name is good enough.
Let's hear the sound of walking.
Walking is part of the song.
A cactus god dreams everything.
I heard about your other god.
I heard it walking.

the golden age of dobby gibson*
  (a slideshow for dobby gibson, b. 1970)

During the Golden Age of Dobby Gibson
the subject senses himself at the center
of the seven directions.

In visions a dark fish swallows the stars.
Then he sees the fish
is merely the hand of a god, wiping clean
a windshield *in front of* the stars.

Dobby Gibson waits for divine guidance.
He knows not to separate god from being.

Meanwhile, the gatherers of his speech carry a handful of flame
from the shore of one word to the shore of the next.

field notes:
During the "listening time," rest is brief.
He can easily find food. Instinctively, he has settled
near the riverbank. There is no sign of
domestic animals, though one might find
the muzzle of a wolf in the back of the refrigerator.

time line:
December 1984. In Northern Finland,
beneath a veil of perpetual darkness,
a tide of birds lies stunned from thoughts of Dobby Gibson.

Now heavy dews gather with proper reverence
beneath the windows of Dobby Gibson.

As we develop our field of study we find that
what is near Dobby Gibson grows more distinct.
So that any investigation of one hour of civilized life
reveals only more Dobby Gibson.

We find that Dobby Gibson inhabits the
symbolic realities we whispered of in graduate school.
But also that the power of Dobby Gibson originates without.
He is a conduit for the placement of our fragile personhood
in the protection of sky and earth.

field notes:
He wears the clothes of a simple man.
The neck supports the head. The feet are rooted.

During the Golden Age, the flora and fauna of Dobby Gibson prosper.
Golden feathers fall upon his dwelling.
When a tree is split by lightning a little story walks out
as an offering from the sky.

Dobby Gibson knows that, similarly, we are veiled
by our external forms.
That the body is sometimes
a miserable equipment we must placate,
the way the sober listen to the drunks
who think they have wings.

field notes:
By firelight, the skull of Dobby Gibson appears robust.
As if seen from the eye of a peacock feather
the mind's expedition into Dobby Gibson grows greener.

Dobby Gibson tells of places beyond the limits of maps.
Of a cattle bone from a cave in southwest Libya,
and its properties of spiritual direction.
How at times the chemical puzzle of being recedes,
and how the keeper of these times is Dobby Gibson.

Undoubtedly, for the visionary, some sort of troublesome
journey to the netherworld ensues.
He either climbs the long rope of the moon's legs
or swims through the underbelly of a deep pond,
carrying back strange hairs from the island of the dead.

But now is also the moment of Dobby Gibson.
Visions, he tells us, *do not happen in time.*

Then Dobby Gibson discusses
the natural hunger of the human eye
for Dobby Gibson.

timeline:
July 1991. The blossoms of Dobby Gibson are just appearing.

He is Dobby Gibson of our subsistence.
He is Dobby Gibson of death medicine.
He is Dobby Gibson of the Region of Dobby Gibson.

In calculations to ensure humanity's well-being,
Dobby Gibson computes the secret of each moment
as a function of the four elements.

The solitude of Dobby Gibson is, of course, like a rain.

Often a layperson approaches Dobby Gibson with questions
such as: What is the origin of the propulsive force
behind the expansion of the universe?
Dobby Gibson tells us: *The answer to almost every question is a song.*

And once monsters sang in the constellations,
sang in the water, sang the name of Dobby Gibson.
Though in human society this name went unspoken.

field notes:
As a taunting gesture, Dobby Gibson eats a serpent.

From the transcripts we discern that one nether region
is inhabited by dogs that hear into the future
and know the great noise of the earth's roasting.

We also know that we are guests in the earth's body,
and its silence may be that which fills with devils, and
the incidental humming of Dobby Gibson may be the releaser.

Dobby Gibson tells us: *The bear is the gorilla of North America.*

Today Dobby Gibson palpitates in all languages.
His mystical work will wash away our sorrows.

timeline:
October 2004. Dobby's friend Jacques Derrida dies in Paris. A
mourning time.

Dobby Gibson tells us: *One makes and loses oneself continuously.*

Dobby Gibson is a man of this world
and eats cooked food
but also belongs to the world above and the world below.
During the Golden Age he travels freely.

timeline:
February 2006. Many Dobby Gibson centers are started to help those
who lack basic cosmic understanding.

Dobby Gibson tells us: *Poetry is how we communicate with the unseen.*

Of the sleeping Dobby Gibson we know little:
it is said that hundreds of starlings murmur about.

Near the end of the Golden Age,
because of the size of his empire,
communication with Dobby Gibson
becomes a lengthier process.

Still, Dobby Gibson tells us: *The eye socket of the halibut migrates.*

Even in times of great burden,
all the bright and brittle things of Earth know him.
His way of life is adopted in widely separate places,
perhaps even microscopically, miles above in Earth's atmosphere.

Dobby Gibson tells us: *Humans have managed to domesticate one insect.*

We have learned that the sleep of Dobby Gibson is "the sleep of Spain."
That it is not easy to see him.
He is just quiet enough to keep warm
among the starlings.

Remember that one of the seven directions is simply
the radiant point of being.

During the Golden Age of Dobby Gibson,
there is, more precisely, a Golden Hour.
A time of miraculous, light-filled speech.

In his court many have awaited the hour.
There are the memorizers of Dobby Gibson.
There are the performers of the sleep of Spain.
There are those who type blindly, hoping to discover his spirit.

But Dobby Gibson is born from nothing,
as ultimately, all is known by the name of nothing.
The fire god knows the sea snail and both are swallowed up.

Do you want now to be asleep
in the ache of your own image?

As you are Dobby Gibson, so I am Dobby Gibson.
As from illusion this world grows dense,
so from the singing and scenery in the mind do we know
ourselves.

Be assured of this guiding principle:
As you are Dobby Gibson, so am I.

*This poem has previously been performed as the golden ages of three other divine
placeholders: rupert wondolowski, best friends forever, and brendan lorber.

in sales

walk the holy land
it is a pilgrimage
giving the leg, taking it away
giving the leg, taking it away

and soot must fall at last on
things-you've-forgotten-the-names-for
as you walk the holy land

one two three

steam is inner knowledge
the chief element of prayer
and soot must fall at last

how is it possible

in sales, when customers
tell you to draw an elephant
you draw a pretzel
and convince them it's an elephant

these are fill-in-the-blank hours

giving the leg, taking it away
giving the leg, taking it away
and
a bad case of grip the handle

well
a superhero has special powers
like the ability to sell
wires repeat the names
I've forgotten the name for
things that repeat

one holy man says
your drug of choice may be flowers or cash or steam

I am in sales   I recite
closed or open
cash or credit

followed by a continuous prayer one two three

sniffing some glue

a salesman draws continuous silence
on a pilgrimage
an outpouring of fill-in-the-blank grace

I try to find the door-to-door dark
now it floats now it doesn't

I try to find more blossoms in
things-I-have-forgotten-the-names-for
like one open prayer
stretched across town

prayer no. 1:
now I wanna sniff some glue
now I wanna have something to do

I could sell you a name for
things that will happen after death
which is stopping

a salesman walks through town
followed by continuous silence

I accept my fill-in-the-blank punishment
the forgotten grip on
the circle I clean
giving the leg, taking it away

well
one holy man has forgotten the name for
painted lines in parking lots
leading to salvation

one two three

a superhero tries to understand

I have forgotten the name for
silence in the hands continuously
and
it is a funny business
following the mind of property

the air full of
things-I've-forgotten-the-names-for

well
all the kids want
painted lines in parking lots
sniffing glue in the
door-to-door hours of salvation

does a salesman fulfill the essential condition of prayer?
you feel a hum answering you
one two three

prayer no. 2:
now I wanna be your dog
now I wanna be your dog

I am in sales   I recite
and
what is holy is mostly sound

well
how is it possible
to convince people
it's an elephant
giving the leg
it's an elephant
taking it away

I have forgotten the name for walking blindly
one two three
cleaning the circle

a salesman walks through town
followed by one two three

when people ask for thirty seconds
of fill-in-the-blank prayer
I convince them
it's a young bird's hum in my hands
it's the continuous silence
in a crack through the earth
it's a fill-in-the-blank need

we carry our equipment
into the door-to-door dusk
but divine law permits no grip on the handle

if you are watching me
I have already rebuilt your interior life
if you are full of tricks
I say one two three
on the surface of your mind
and
if you have forgotten the names of things
I have them in my briefcase

well
with all my strength
I have forgotten the name for
the empty museum in my body
the fill-in-the-blank need
I cannot sell

prayer no. 3:
should I stay or should I go
should I stay or should I go

a great force holds things down
it makes you tired
where no one can see
one two three

still another blocked door
upside down at the bottom of a prayer
maybe you have a tin one

when you smell
a prayer blossoming in the storefront reflection
I say
pluck it

I say
sometimes on a pilgrimage
you hear the hum

in sales soot must fall at last
followed by the name for
the circle you clean
one two three

I have forgotten the name for
continuous silence in shop windows
or salvation through interior life

a superhero tries
to carry what is holy
into the door-to-door dusk

you must not repeat
the name for things you didn't know were there
the name for secrets inside a box
the name for little image on the wall

you must not
until I walk the roadside
with the circle
saying
one two three
it's an elephant

obedience

It is better to sleep upstairs
in the world of dreams.
Almost shining in the sky.

My parents have never told me
one dream they've had.
When daylight moves in, a settlement,
the dream travels by dog.
It is a dog in the shape of a dog.

In a dream my parents finally tell me
one dream they've had.
Then I sit up in bed and dream I
sit up in bed
telling my wife about a dream I had
with a dog in it.

My father yells up the stairs
I had a dream, I had a dream.

Then I look out the window
and see a space on the sidewalk
where a dog just was.
The dog that sleeps when I am awake
and wakes up running when I fall asleep.

Later, in the shower,
I put my mouth to the nozzle

and I am a dog.
What if my parents
have never had one dream?

I sit up in bed
almost shining in the sky
and tell my wife about a dream.
Then downstairs in the shower
I am a dog, distracting myself
from the other thing I am becoming.

My dreamless father shouts up the stairs.
He can't walk anymore,
he is in my dream.
He will have to travel by dog.

the making of the golden age of dobby gibson
> *(a DVD extra)*

First, we wore conservative suits.
Second, we assumed that no part of the universe
was more aware of itself than any other part.

Then we asked:
What information is there about Dobby Gibson?

In the beginning we stayed within the veil of science.
But the small opening in symbolic communication
trapped us on the path of our feelings.
All we had was a theoretical construct based on inferences.

Then we asked, "What is lost for each of us
by not being Dobby Gibson?"

We knew the answer was made of a dazzling light!

So, to consider Dobby Gibson, we first studied
the origin of speech.

We divined the impossible pre-moments of Dobby Gibson.
We washed and washed the husk of cognition
and sifted our thoughts of Dobby Gibson as if they were minute gems.

Evidence of a Golden Age was everywhere.

To make the Golden Age visible
we chose between the two methods of "seeing":
pilgrimage and hallucinogenic trance.

We held small, charmed stones.
We closed our eyes and saw fields of radiant being.
We made a thought Dobby Gibson and a toy Dobby Gibson.

Then we asked, *Has our study of Dobby Gibson been impeded
by the presence of taboos?*

Our text took shape in its nonconscious mode.
We decided it did not matter whether Dobby Gibson
was conscious of anything at all.

Then we asked ourselves, *Do we love Dobby Gibson?*
For without love we are distracted.
Then as if from deliverance by celestial bird
whatever was both human and divine came before us
and we examined each word as a seed spit into the skull.

Next, by eating roots we discovered a truth—
events that did not exist still had great power.

After a series of these extra-smooth late-night highs
the trance to seek Dobby Gibson
began to seek us. Our vision formed
as one trail on the path of human light.

At another level of cognition
Dobby Gibson appeared within us.

In the trance, each of these thoughts
became a living temple to be entered,
each a being that changed from
one matterless state to another.

We understood that the business of making Dobby Gibson
had fallen into the usual cooperative pattern.
That we would not have been human
if we weren't interested in Dobby Gibson.

We obeyed the telepathic command of the original search,
the hundreds of astrologers
locating the origin of speech
and the visions of mouths that kiss at our hearts.

Our text formed as a skeleton of the living thought.

We continued to ignore the ordinary trick of having a body
and how it fills with hours.
A fire appeared in our heads as a smile.
We stood on this thin bridge.

Then the hero arrived.

the lawrence welk diaries

(a poem in four scenes)

CHARACTERS

(in order of appearance)

Lawrence Welk . . . . I'm tiny, I'm an acorn.
Michel Foucault . . . . listened like a dog
Eartha Kitt . . . . the air untied from within a knot
Sam Shepard . . . . changed shape to avoid questions

SYNOPSIS OF SCENES

I psalmody (establish the question)
II crack, crackle (establish the method of inquiry)
III bad news, Santa (have the experience)
IV juke(box) (report the transmutation)

COSTUMES: all dressed in visions flowing from an unknown
correspondent, in mockery of the bright skin of the
pomegranate, in memory of a harvest, of a railroad clerk, of a
name marked on boxes with drops of molten wax, rewards
gathered as after a flood and almost used as a battle cry.

SCENE I *evening, four people around a fire in a wolf field, it's the*
back-to-the-viscera movement with the basic substance of life
trucked across the interstate and raised up as in holy visions of
disease-serving gifts, a lump that sings between intelligent thoughts

LW: In North Dakota I heard a pony
count handclaps through dirty teeth and
I understood, the gayer the lights, the
better the luck; we were all tripping
on that tour. I don't see getting drowned.
I don't see looking unlovely. It's Mother's fault.
The hundredth bang, very sore, it makes
me smaller, I'll live on, I'll nude, I'll
swerve notes until the old Greek scales
fall from our eyes. As the pumping organ
cannot speak, I can guarantee you love.

MF: All I can think about is Yoko Ono.
I'm down to the pattern of human speech
that can boil water; Yoko lives her
ninety-nine meanings and falls apart, all in one
note, man. I get crazy, the protocol of
shifting forms slips into the open sea.

LW: I'm authorized to be lazy. I took
four pages of notes on a little slipper of
fur. In '53 we made dugout caves and
diminished the downbeat. This generation
is the flower operator. I never heard of them.

EK: Gentlemen, the question is how our
song makes the flower become noticeable,
the flower that has bloomed in the air
since day one, since the word.

SCENE II *the violent rush of birds in all five senses, and death the*
flower of lasting just another trail put together in a line of blow
angling into the sky; the fire burns down

EK: A swift little boat formed a wound in
the sea, are you following? The infant
has traveled through it and become a
retailer, full of sour and stirring up.
Larry, Mikey, I'm just talking shit.

MF: Yoko. Ono.

LW: Right, and a dictionary seems to
have two heads when soaked in water.
But we gotta think. We'll show them
what it means to burst a jockey with
just brainwaves. *Pow!* and riding on the
horse is an enormous flower. Fuckin' A.

SCENE III *inside the trailer, poison at every meal and delight in a task*
soiled by the stars, kerosene lamp applied literally by the forms above

SS: I was with Yoko and we hurried
through the keyhole, the one that allures,
the ardent desires, the rumble of
distant drums.

MF: Fuckin' A.

SS: Eartha, the sideshows in Australia
were done Irish style, with continuous
tongue, and it was suggested to pinch,
to bite, to join the paths of travelers.

LW: Pass.

SCENE IV *sunrise and the four squint at something drawn on a
card to bring back news from the dead, a light raised into flower by
the art of kindling; we all squint to read the news from an unseen
mind brightened by rubbing, and then the card goes blank*

MF: The universe is a party.

LW: The sea holding a ship in a mistaken thought,
buckling, bringing together, that's the birth of
our flower's name, the universal dwelling of
our work is a golden cloth, laid upon the
wilderness for a constant flow of pilgrims,
concentrating on the pure adventure of the
slug's path, *dig that*. Pass.

EK: To fight sleep, to always see sleep as the enemy,
as a child does. To hum the world's directions
and not know it. To shelter another meaning for hell
against the raw heckle of the lord and grow it
to fruition in the limbs of the sea. To beget, this is
our reward on Earth translated into seafoam, hence
the halo and sometimes we call the result *linoleum*.

SS: Friends, today appeared. As the sancta gradalis.
Are we pure enough animals to be eaten on holy days?
Celestial Mother style? Are we not the bird ravished by the
smear of god that forms a snap of fingers?
I call on your delight in licorice, its medicine paste,
to hear by picking up grains; to swim by reading
ashes in a mirror; to find us by following the
altar smoke and by turning at random to a page,
naming the wind with cake dough. We bathe in you.
We leap into flower and are born together, fuckin' A.

four figures pass across a flower rubbed down by
constant use. amid sound from the gossip of roads
and the quiet voice of the animal towed in silhouette
behind the sun, the four name the axis of the sky then
tip on the brink of action; each direction touches
its flower and flies away.

categories of being cloud man

∞

A gatherer on the riverbank
waits for floating bodies.
Each body carries its dream downriver.

Cloud Man sleeps beneath the snow, like a seed.

He thinks of many grasshoppers
burrowed into earth, having many dreams.

He makes one hole the size of a dead body,
then one space around the hole for his life.

∞

In a dream Cloud Man sleeps inside an egg
and grows a beak to hatch from the frozen shell.

What luck, he knows,
to dream-speak in bone language,
as to another being, as to time.

But a beak is not really a bone, he thinks, *more like
a toenail that sings.*

He waits through night in a crust of furs.

∞

In sleep he invents a slow city
that grows like snow along a riverbank.
He understands, once you leave the dream-egg,
it's broken. There's no way to unknow it.

All night a breath rolls over the top
of Cloud Man. One breath and the next.

In a dream he sees a beak
on the front of a locomotive
eating and whistling through the night.
The city of his dream chokes forward.
The river scrapes along its bed.

In sleep, Cloud Man knows one silence from another.
He dreams each furrow as a circle, plowed into time.

∞

When he wakes, he says
There is more to life than heartbreak.
Says, *A cloud has no true center.*

The stars age away,
Cloud Man gives up and lives
or he dies and
hatches from snow to live again.

He surfaces, blind, into
a world without fat.
His death is faithful to him.
He thanks the mothers of speech

who have awakened him
from his dream-egg.

It's an empty walk back to the people.
A blur, a trail of sideways steps.
Says *I have slept once and left a city in my wake.*

∞

During the hoarding time that follows,
roads harden into ways of thinking.
Pike are afraid to swim to the surface.

Today we live his dream, we rise again, we give up.
Thin clouds reflect on glass buildings.

Roads plow forward over the sleeping gatherers.
We rise again.
Cloud Man has stepped off the earth.
Cloud Man is at a door.
We rise again and follow our own footprints to the river.

∞

What must it be to take the form of a toad or bird?
Cloud Man incubates.
It's an empty walk through each age of the earth.

The hibernating animals make great changes occur
but do not change themselves. They dream.

Cloud man considers

the speck of dust he is becoming,
seed for one drop of rain.

Considers the namelessness that encased his sleep
and the sleep itself.
How the flower matures and dies into seed.

"At this point it is only necessary to say 'and so on.'"
        (Fred Hoyle)
One hole for sleep, one space around the hole for this dream.

∞

In the book of each day, footprints
establish their numbers and
one number has been established for Cloud Man.

We have given up.
Still, heat reaches the earth from two directions
                (outside and inside)
and our heart's ease blooms through summer.

Cloud Man sees in himself some dust and water
from a city of dried seeds.

Says, *as long as you are not death
I will sleep next to you.*
At night there is often stirring in the deep mud,
the mystery of life below ground.

∞

Today a cloud rises from each home,
circle into square, then dissolves
and returns, square into circle.

Our river washes one mind into another.
On the far bank the dream-clouds unknot.
The gatherer waves, his hand on fire.

Cloud Man moves against the current.

Says, *you don't know the name of my name.*
Says, *the earth hears me.*

the game of zero

in the dream I dreamt
the child said,
"when I touch this tree you have to die"
so I fell down

out of one dream into another
alone through darkness
through blank leagues of water
to clear trees in glare sun

half-woken foot feels for a rock
in dull coils of sleep

I hear the child speak
fall down again
nerve endings gray

I'm in a house with a bone chimney
this darkness
the kingdom of pregnancy

I believe I was the child's dream
also the trees and sky and room and breath
surrounding the dream

over waves of neurochemistry
I stayed with the child
for lifetimes
I stayed as long as possible

I was a real character in that universe
a fat sparrow even said my name
but the child still put its hand on the tree.

abstract order

rabbit

  or, the disenchantment

1: emergence

A little bunny rabbit appears, ready to be worshipped in the
bright world. How does matter become a bunny rabbit? Does life-
force climb the skin of our village? Maybe our longing made
supernatural offspring. They flash into the open-country wonder
of our time. Who will chant the rabbit children into being now?
When I was a child, rabbits rang by the riverside, rabbits wiser
than east or west. Then our little bunny brothers chewed off some
hands. Who is on moonwatch for little bunny rabbits tonight?
Who will make sure old age yellows the lives of the new old
rabbits?

2: intention

A county judge fears the little bunny rabbit has gnawed through
twilight to eat our children. Probably the original darkness will
follow. The little bunny rabbit sings the life of coming out. Its
song links our feelings together like roots or vines. The little
bunny rabbit steps into a blizzard of our memories. Will we ravel
into some collaborative beast? We will know too many words. The
little bunny rabbit, round like dusk, gathers us howling in a hot
rush of loam, gathers us in a seed pouch as we boil at our desks.
The little bunny rabbit recognizes himself in laughter from the
burrows and dens, from the patient river, the patient salt. The
little bunny rabbit has probably eaten a child or two.

3. union

Let's try to talk to the little bunny rabbit. Let's see who it is. Well, the little bunny rabbit is actually a replica of the primary brain, which is all laughs. Is this because of universal development toward complexity? The night before, no little bunny rabbit. Tonight, bunnies everywhere, freshly thought, could be a new wonder. Little bunny rabbit in the feather we speak to. In the pulsing attractions. In the pond alive. Little bunny rabbit buried at the bottom of a fire, let's talk.

4: spectacle

On Thursdays we take miracle lessons from the little bunny rabbit. First, two old men find the only smoke child in the park and bring it to the courthouse. The hot hovering judge clears the dusky glass. Rain downwind, the gleaming cupola. Children eat the bells, lightning breaks green, there is moon pressure. The judge, too, is like a hot little bunny rabbit. During the first lesson, the little bunny rabbit is simply a vibration in the nervous system. But that's enough of a miracle.

5: revelation

Now there waits a little bunny rabbit at the edge of space. It is *our own salvia bunny.* It stands, paws up, like a cop! A cop! Who suddenly has the head and claws of a rabbit and moves cop-like toward us. Please concentrate, someone is being a cop. But the little bunny rabbit dissolves into neon and becomes a cave. In the cave there's an audience; they keep changing the shapes of their heads. Now they're popcorn-headed people. Now their heads flatten into background. Now the little bunny rabbit appears and speaks: *I grew from an original darkness following time-space.* Are you the audience or the cave or the rabbit? Don't trust anyone with your answer.

6: calling

The little bunny rabbit's dreams have their own motors. If we ever stop kissing we'll probably get stuck winding them. The little bunny rabbit watches our supernatural kiss from the blue and white windows of the spirits. The little bunny rabbit becomes pregnant with music. We put a horn on the head of our kiss and listen. How many bunnies do we hear? They must be splitting themselves in two! They must be dropping from a fantastic tree! The little bunny rabbits understand calculus. A sun and moon take shape. How are we being tricked now? Did we accidentally become the motors?

7: proliferation

It turns out there's a rabbit buried beneath the rabbit. It turns out there's another rabbit buried *inside* the rabbit. Out of the utterly aimless confusion rabbits ring. Out of the wounded-leaning night rabbits vibrate beneath rabbits and the thunder of their victory keeps us prisoner. They are just always doing it. The outward vessel of the little bunny rabbit carries enthusiasms through the town and the town is a maze of silence. We want a miracle to assert itself. Candles burn in the dark interior of our plan for heaven. It turns out there's a rabbit buried in the town's silence. We know our plan for heaven must now include little bunny rabbits.

8: conveyance

In the middle of their swollen bodies, the little bunny rabbits smell of crust and scream of the high blue sky. The chewing of children forms a magic. Our fingertips read the word in a rabbit's stomach. It is a magic to save the children from the fluttering cares of their own interiors. Also for rabbits to protect the satisfied townspeople from the wrong joy. And for the old old rabbits to bring themselves to spiritual self-defense. Trees and streams are citizens. The little bunny rabbits drag us toward a cathedral. Why do we use hot water to discover ourselves, and why can't we use little bunny rabbits? Oh how the village trees are part of our play tonight.

9: conjuring

Outside the courthouse little bunny rabbit brides and grooms stream through the bitter June. Pink bone rain pocks the magical building. Tonight we sleep to the tingling of little bunny rabbit matter. Courtroom officials have already scrubbed the blood walk. A miracle chopper there aches to judge little bunny rabbits. Torchlight sours, hush in the bird sizzle. If we are secret beasts kept by rabbit gods we have failed them. Evil thrills radiate from the cupola. Little bunny rabbits always doing it by the dark window, our blood-heavy heads startled by their kitchen rhythms tunneling inward. We hear their guts tick.

10: disappearance

The little bunny rabbit cycle goes *shine, arrive, rinse*. They exit our town as regular rabbits and the judges smile kindly. Each judge sways a trophy bag of pain between his legs. The deeper difficulties of enchantment have blown from our heads. Lot sixty-three contains no rabbits. Our vacant woods produce an empty whistle. Above us the chain of tangled dragonfly light might be a pollution now. Our magnetism remains undeveloped in the bountiful autumn, our moon resembles a concrete pupil. Judges stare into the river; the fish are next. The empty whistle. Forward speed burns the leaves black. The rabbits are still gods, but not our gods.

11: following

The unknown attractor pulling us toward the end of time may be a rabbit. But if we call out for a little bunny rabbit now we'll get mythical guilt. Cruel language will bend the brain. Out dark windows now there's a horse of human skulls washed in milk. The next generation of animals sleeps in a ghost. Our children will see little bunny rabbit stories hovering above our love space. Their eyes will go flying, their lit dreams will go aglow, past firelight will unspool in the memory house. Telepathic rabbits, humped in the grass, tell what was. How the inner lining of skin breathes. How resistance softens and molds a lump in rain.

12: recollection

We say the first little bunny rabbit looms in the void. Or we blaze up in wonder. The light of us comes toward us in a rabbit shape. No one stands guard by the river, mind flipping. The trick is now that we know the trick. We're left stroking hulls of ruined air. Hurry, something is happening. We've been educated by rabbits to see our damage repeat damage like a machine. They are gone with our almost fullness. No, an evaporator judge took our fullness. It's already unclear. We are pregnant with passive nature. A rabbit used to do what only a god does now. Remember?

further
geographies

map

It's a long way from cloud to rabbit
but not so far from bicycle to cloud.
To get from cactus to bicycle
you have to go through feather.
Ghost leads to cactus.
River is carried to ghost by dog.
From rabbit, proceed to yam,
then to river. It will take a long time
to get from bicycle to dog, all the way
through cloud, rabbit, yam, and river.
If we could go backward we could
get from rabbit to feather faster.
We can never go backward.

cloud calling for beginners

for, and from, Sun Yung Shin

I.

The first surprise is the egg,
its rhythm of possible beings, its lack of nation.
Then the baby made of ordinary fire,
all the parts of a flower alive and fingerprinted
in its speech. Then the naming song of the mother.

What is the purpose of observing children?
Only what is seen and heard.

II.

Aztecs divined us in bowls of water.
Their children daydreamed the heads of our children,
each self a zero in a mouth of time.
They watched us choose between dream and being
then enter the egg that has no wild ancestor,
our empty Cadillac, the human dark.

Today some wise asker, offstage, from the bottom of a pond:
And where are you from?
Each even tone of being like
a white room a god steps out of, and another,
then a sense of sudden rain filling time.

III.

Tomorrow's children march through an empty factory
and lie down to dream us in a book of shivers.
We are one sea of memory happening through
a mouth in winter, one calm afternoon nap
with a fly in the window, one adult entering
the hairy weather of the self, never to return.

Today we have so many mothers
sewing heaven to earth, back and forth.
The child hides in a zero that hides
in the husband, who crouches in
a bundle of wood and is lifted to the sky.

IV.

To be human, to love,
to wonder where they get their T-shirts,
to sweep a hand beneath the levitator,
to get better,
to have four legs in a dream,
to be in a warm spot and say, "I'm in a warm spot"
as in the current layer of people scraping over earth,
as in a cloud calling for beginners,
in which the vapor bodies are cared for,
in which a dream pounds, and then
to graze as witnesses over each child's pasture,
to heat the shivering birds,
to be located and remember their song
and how to say it.

V.

Where we return, sewn to earth,
a child appears, and another,
back and forth they go.

It is said that the children are carried
to the woodcutter's temple, that when
their threads descend from the sky
at midnight, that is awareness.
And where are you from?

the number of heaven and earth

They stole chickens and
slaughtered cows
they castrated pigs
they cut the tails off piglets
they followed deer through the woods
shot them in their necks
they put out traps
they raised lambs then slit their throats
they hung animals upside down in their barns
the blood drained out
their guts were baskets
they carried babies or carried bread
downriver to grandmother's gut
in the fall they slaughtered and they boiled meat
they canned the meat and stored it
in root cellars in shelved rows
and other parts, even brains
they used for sausage
and they tied horses to iron equipment
and whipped them
while the dogs just ran free
they put meat in a clearing
and waited for a bear
all of this meat is how I am

      my great-grandfather stole three chickens
      he was put in jail
      he got out had a stroke

         then he could only swear
         only from half his face
         his wife lost her mind, was
      "committed" but when he died
         she "came out of it"
         lived for years
         never stole chickens

they caught fish and slid steel knives
into their bellies
they dreamt of animals
the animal terror went into their bodies
and they too lost their minds
coyotes came to speak to them
they killed other people
as they were told to
they kidnapped a Lakota woman
it was winter there was so much snow
and nothing to kill
they survived on potatoes and
canned meat and canned pears
so that I was born

         and one day a rabbit bit the tip off my finger
         and chewed it up
         so we killed the rabbit

some of them lived with mules in Kentucky
or horses in Massachusetts
some of them turned their front yards
into pig wallows in Iowa

and they kept slaughtering
they bought guns and sows
and killed who they were told to kill
and made whiskey
and killed rabbits and raccoon and foxes
they poached and ran
or later drove their cars into ditches
and more of them went to jail
they wanted sex and families
they wanted to slaughter more animals
even a horse in the worst of times
they were ready
in their root cellars
and they sang about food and animals
they played guitars by the stove
or on porches
and more animals died and became songs
meat dripping everywhere
and I got here and began eating

     this morning I saw a rabbit in the driveway
     I saw its beautiful eye
     it was feminine
     it carried a baby it carried bread
     its eye was a womb
     I was given a heart-shaped basket
     made from dried plants
     and I rode it down the river
     I thought *who is riding in the basket*
     it feels like no one
     the incinerator came on at dusk

in the old yellow sky
and wolf-children came out
their hair gone poisonous
the people grew tired of raising them
and rubbing pollen on their bodies
grew tired of how years
run together after dark

they kept their bodies warm to stay alive
they cut down trees
and burned them to boil water
they shaved the sheep
they spun and wove the wool
children watched the looms fill
they had to keep warm
and some of them burned animal shit
some burned oil from the ground
or oil from giant whales
hauled onto boats and hacked to pieces
and the chimneys glowed hot
the lanterns glowed
children slept near whatever could burn
the adults killed to stay warm
they killed to eat
they burned lost people passing through
and the children watched their faces melt

he has a face problem
there's the seed of a face in there
all withered
someone check his teeth

looks like the kind of person
to squish in a machine
press the juice out of
rip apart with horses
pour boiling water onto
shoot metal into
tell him to keep moving
or we'll set him afire

they wanted to stay warm
they wanted to make more children
the rivers flooded
they were alive but winter came on
night came too and they wrote letters
someone lit a candle
the church bell froze
a crow perched on the chimney meant
someone would die
a white dog on the road at night
was a spirit
a woodpecker at the window
meant prosperity
a coyote in the yard
meant bad luck and a hard winter
souls inhabited the fires
ancestors spoke from the mouths of fish
the cemetery glowed at night
an elk wandered up to the house
to deliver its message
how fire keeps the busy spirits away
sunlight in the pines

wild turkeys half-mad along the road
long lines of eggs and mothers and
sunlight in their feathers
each evidence of glowing sound
mind expansion practice dream
the squirrel alive and
the hawk in its piece of sky
and they prayed for sanctuary
they dreamt of the number twelve
and of twelve gears
turning this world
through the levels of urge
and in their dreams
where celestial fruits fell
into twelve tributaries
they prayed to be absorbed
by the divine
but instead they woke up
and drank whiskey
and wanted to fight
they distilled moonshine
in Kentucky
they took amphetamines and kept working
kept killing
the word was sacred
so they didn't speak
they built El Dorado
they built industrial parks
on the graves of each other
they built flashbulbs and stark faces
they built orchards and winding roads

and shutters for the windows
of homes they built or stole
and they built a word for us
they called us the future
and they kept killing
they got to twelve and they started over
the future was both heaven and earth
the gods the months the stars
a spiral of twelve
a fulfillment
an eating sound.

oyster meditation

the kind of love with your hands in your pocket love
the kind of bedroom in wisconsin
the leaving of a possible dawn
where within us an idiot drops a stone

in the bedroom I see a light that kind of love
maybe the question of god kind of wisconsin love

or *please do,* saying it alone afterward
please do in wisconsin

a certain smaller attitude is necessary
in the field of love-thinking
that kind of question you answer with *please do*
or your hands

I try to understand without using my mind
a person's love-thinking could have the ability
to be as inward as an old oyster

I try to in love understand
to extract *mystical unity* from cell walls

the internal orator is as permissive as a drifting rowboat
through the mind's unbearable grain
I try to answer the question with food in my hands
with my mind saying it alone
the question of god in my body

in a pocket of bedroom where *mystical unity*
first rises
I try to be the kind of god in an old oyster
without using my mind

to answer the question of how thinking "sees"
and say it alone until I see a light

drug culture

there is at least one room with no doors
it is father
after the stroke
we squeeze his toes and stare through the ice
we call selfishly for our great surprise
bring back fire or a talking fish
but father's job is to make a curse

I buy something and it disappears
the light changes; I buy it again a hundred times
I buy more *property;* it disappears
the empty space fills with drug
then a hundred tones of light

the electricity has gone out
we build a fire
we call it the brain
we stand around and watch it think
all this thinking fell to earth
I look up at the clouds
forget they are clouds

who slept in my bed all those years
was I even dreaming
was my body a catalog a season
deep kissing outside under the trees
what is work
what do we do at work

I go downstairs what can I buy here
I make a list of drugs and see
a lime vanish then a glass of water
each breath a moon breath

I am alone
except for three maple trees
two outside the window
one inside the drug

I go into the kitchen
to get some light; it disappears
suddenly the Buddha head
is back in the potato bin

I can't say words
before they disappear
the only way out of the drug is
the paleolithic amber way

think of the drug as home
into this drug there flows a little brook
a pastoral state of affairs
leaves fall into my home

each time the dog barks
a light goes on it must be
my light coming back
such joy in a single night, deep night
an erotic sentence of lamentation
not in earth language
spoken by cloud or fire

I finally see myself
in the church bells
with unnamed people
luminous strangers in drug space
and we're inside them
a sugar dream
tendrils in a mouth
a lamentation of disappearing light

there is no door
we're in drug culture now
it's polydeviant
we must wear father bravely
as he disappears

occupant

last night I dreamt   my left hand was distortion

          I needed someone   a shadow

                    to perform

          in a misty basement   a bacterial concert

also dreaming itself was performance

               the audience   colder and closer   in seedlight

                              then the quiet beaching of the dream

          room like a fountain the moon sprang from
                         help me wake

                    walk in a dark house thinking   who will wake me

I have a desk   I'll never find it in all this luxury

          oh yes   tonight we have to throw the baby

                                        into the bonfire
waking up is never not performance

               in the stairway

          a worm rises from my eye   turns to smoke

               it's terrible   I have to build the fire

     in the dark   with breath

someone hands me the baby   it's already covered in napalm

there are three rules
     1. everything that happens is the performance
     2. every reaction is a true reaction
     3. a dream is real

right-hand distortion now   left-hand music of flies

         who is the audience for a dream
            in the stairway

I hear there is a war on drugs
       as in take one of these   write down what you feel

     relinquish all grasping   all letting go

         I perform moon audience

            down the stairs

someone says, "I just put in two weeks' notice   at my dream

   it was a bank job   they made me burn babies"

burning up

Dawn came and there was something like a great ear
behind the sun.
Ashes drifted down though nothing had burned.
I wanted to shine like a fish.

Supposedly there are people who
will not burn in a fire.
Biblical people.

I carried my bucket.
Dead men pumped water from
the center of the earth.
We all drank it.

More ashes arrived.
We caught them on our tongues,
angels of next time receiving the body.

The earth tumbled then,
the pump handle creaked.

When soldiers came, we ran.
Like always.
I did a snake dance into the culvert.
Soldiers were afraid of ghosts.

A tongue is like a fish worn dull,
shine gone.

Day after day pieces of wood
floated down the river.
What were they building down there, at the end?

They were building a cross.
They were building a bird to fly us out.
They were building a new city
for the dead to lead from
and the soldiers were blind to it.

By noon the ghosts were gone.
The pump handle creaked, but no water.
When the soldiers came back I changed.

I became an angel of next time.
I said the words and
scales fell from my fish tongue
but the giant ear was stone.
Soldiers drifted like ashes.

I told them:
Downriver they build
wings that will not burn in a fire
and you are right to hide.
Put down your guns.

Soldiers put us in trucks
and took us downriver to become ashes.
The shine stopped.
The giant ear heard everything but
there was no mouth to speak.

In the cage, we counted.
Clouds.
Men.
Hours.
Flies rose from the ash piles.

We counted screams.
A body floated downriver.

Dawn came and men
with no eyes talked
to the giant ear.
Roadside men who
lay dead in a snake dance.

The fireproof bird might rise
tomorrow or never.
All believed in it.
It rained or it would
never rain.

We counted Americans.
Flies performed their math on the dead.
We counted silences.

The sun had one voice
and the river had one voice.
Burnt people dropped from trees.

We slept to the rustling
of boots through weeds

and I remembered the water
of a dead nun's voice.

We were all floating downriver.
Dawn came.
We knew nothing and they shot
half of us, with American guns.

At the sound of it we forgot.
We listened to the river.
Each gunshot carried by water
to dazzle the great ear.

That night I became a snake.
I slipped between the beams.
Crawled among the dead.

I followed the sound of bells.
Downriver.
The soldiers could not count
or didn't care to.
The river counted to one
forever
in its long voice.

Some snakes do not end.
Mythical snakes.
I passed a village.

Downriver there was nothing
except ashes.

The village boiled in silence.
A snake does not scream.

The choices were:
Death.
Torture.
Become a snake.

Forest creatures swam in blood.
My voice drifted past,
covered by the long scar of forgetting.

I know the great ear turned.
That ghosts rose and began their work.
That voices fell from the trees.

I remain in snake form.
I whisper instructions to the great ear
following each little death.

Because now we are ready.
We have so many ashes
for our bird to rise from.

We have a sound to carry us
home, the river's one voice
singing all day to a giant ear.

what we knew and what we decided and what we built
 (guerilla warfare)

1.

We wanted to capture believers and untorture them.
We knew that money bent inside other money so
we decided to use a trapeze. What else could flicker?
Our roadblock flickered with ghouls and hoofbeats.
We sat still to watch the edgings of leaves.
Somewhere in our moonlight treks a drug culture
stalked invisible senators through the blackbird calls.
Treetops said wavebands. Our trapeze
was a timekeeper and it could trapeze anything.
We surrounded camp with our hoarded babysitter teeth.
Someone lit the pipe arm.
Maybe a ghoul girl missing her toothbrush.
Then we heard office chairs, the fatherland
sliding awake; we knew the motherland was everything.
We stalked the lobbyists through the whiteboards.
Shags moved easterner.
We knew invisible moneylight could flicker us awake too.
We needed a towrope.
None of us understood the woodpeckers.

2.

We thought our daydream might flicker.
We knew that airship death bent inside their tremors.
Green leaves could flame into simple directives.
We needed to carry what they said through the toxin.
No one could turn backdrop ever.

We knew somewhere in the trenches republicans dangled meth lotion.
We decided to watch what was said through the toy.
We built an altimeter.
Someone lit a firebomb.
We heard forces somewhere in the ventricles
and saw daredevils inside light-years.
The faun slid into simulation.
Shallows moved ebb. The creosote flickered.
We built a small firecracker-in-waiting,
an altitude. Were we inside a bud? It was illegal.
Someone lit the firecracker in the trendsetters' mope warehouse.
We decided to set a travesty.
Then for a while the motorbike was everything.
Our travesty was sin and it could travesty anything.
We built a small fire-eater-in-waiting,
we built a gigolo gland.
We heard singing from the fjords of psychedelic Norway.

    3.
We knew deadlines in the guts
and eyewitnesses masked in handkerchiefs
and we knew trespassers and decided
now the motorcade film was everything.
Shame moved ecclesiastic.
A crest flickered and might have been gills
so we built a collection of gill glass.
We needed a walkabout.
We built a small republican-in-waiting.
Of course someone lit the republican.
We saw shining in the trestles and we sat still.
Green leaves could flicker into sinew.

We might need to carry what was said
down to the creek in our tracksuits.
Then we heard budget forecasts.
Somewhere in the wattage vomit flickered.
We sat still and our fears slid awake
and this time we needed a walkie-talkie.
A crewman signaled to our underground farm
and we surrounded the workstations.
Each guerilla picked up
an international observer hammer.
We were inside the warhead;
we were inside the republicans.
We talked smack and then struck.

post-historic

Some enemies are meant to be worn.
Certain animals flourish on cave walls.
The pigeon-lady has painted a leaf.

Suddenly, a bone flute and the depth of being alive,
the hand of space blossoms a moon,
lingering to drink for a while
and monkey-boy and pigeon-lady have conceived.
They have given birth to a typewriter.

The first page of life.

The typed letter: A.

In the ruins of this secret drug, monkey-boy
produces many   two-dimensional maps
of the brain as a dried-up lake bed.

Pigeon-lady is a bird's nest tonight
                  and tonight nests
are portraits everyone here flowers by.

The next world asks.

We are guests within a vast abandoned being.

At the shrine of the thirty-four arms
monkey-boys speak   and give off no light,
the insect call of capital chirps.

Many pages into life: a code develops.
Now the ajar have a limitless view of clappers in harmony,
                              making the earth's heat beat.

Monkey-boy asks sixteen questions in a mountain accent
until sleep
and a scientific dream of recorded fog descends.

                 what the pigeon-lady knew:

The light of the world was not over.
The light of the world was not whole.

Now monkey-boy has slept on a fish
and the fish has dreamt.

                 The river's marrow is an endless cave.
                 Its moon is the sun and its sun is the moon.
                 At evening, past and present
                 flow over the city of fish.

Part of the typewriter is actually a train.
A flood of silk fills the valley.

From where the animals sit it seems
life in a tree faces the whole day.

The tree is named for a ghost story
in which the acres traveled by a bell
fill with reverberations of spirit
whose only real enemy is man.

The tree never speaks again.

Monkey-boy and pigeon-lady discover
that their typewriter is making up the world.

From sparrow to sparrow, waves of counterdream ripple.
The other side of each page of our world is blank.

So one god is put into storage and
the pigeon-lady who gives us ordinary suffering
from her distant tree
calls up a cloud of dust.

Monkey-boy is half-buried in the ground.

Age of grape seeds.
Age of sewing.

Pigeon-lady cannot work forever
along the natural path of an arm to a tool,
she may join the mint family
and hope that a wolf
transports her seeds north.

The last archer prepares to shoot himself.
Caribou-man falls under the weight of his own antlers.

It is late when a strange skull appears on the lake bed.
Upside down. Almost a nest.
It irritates the spirit of pigeon-lady.

Seals and swans and salmon migrate
back and forth
to get rid of their language.

Groups of algae begin to practice determinism.

The skull resembles a boat.
Resembles a trap.
Rain falls into its cup.

In the evening of the last hot day,
as sunlight crosses over shelters of the ancestors,
the fire at the mouth of the cave fades.

The impermanent animal that kept history
returns into earth by tunnel, toward
the memory of its comet.

Due to either human activity or the burrowing of animals,
the typewriter dies.
The sixteen questions die.
The page is left half-finished.

Then a wash of silence covers the lake bed,
and everything that is in the world now
crawls out from the skull.

acknowledgments

Gratefulness and love to the editors who have published some of these poems previously:

- *Altered Scale:* excerpts from "pre-occupation"
- *Conduit:* "obedience" & "cloud calling for beginners"
- *Esque:* "prayer for dropouts" & "what we knew and what we decided and what we built"
- *Fairy Tale Review:* "a brief tour of string quartet no. 3 by karel husa"
- *forklift, OH:* "the golden age of dobby gibson" & "the making of the golden age of dobby gibson"
- *Fuori:* "first impression"
- *Handsome:* "post-historic"
- *jubilat:* "burning up"
- *Mary:* "occupant"
- *Poetry City,* USA, vol. 3: "the number of heaven and earth"
- *Post Road:* "in sales"
- *Revolver:* "drug culture"
- *Shattered Wig Review:* "ode to mescaline" & "map"
- *Tammy:* "oyster meditation"
- *Thin Coyote:* "first impression"
- *WinteRed Press:* "the lawrence welk diaries"

Thank you to those who helped me write these poems and make this book: Sarah Fox again & again, Jeffrey Little, Dobby Gibson, Jordan Roeder, Jeff Skemp, Astronaut Cooper's Parade, Rupert Wondolowski & *Shattered Wig Review,* Nora Wynn, Michelle Filkins & Chris Watercott & the whole Spout gang, Paula Cisewski, Jack Walsh, Christopher Jones, the Knox Writer's House, Lit Kids everywhere, Margaret Miles, Fred Schmalz, Theo Page, Paul & Julie Lindner, Felix, Al & Yoma Colburn, and of course everyone at Coffee House Press—especially Chris Fischbach, Erika Stevens, and Anitra Budd. Thank you.

The creation of some of these poems was also aided by grants from the Minnesota State Arts Board and the Jerome Foundation, to whom I extend my deep gratitude.

COFFEE HOUSE PRESS

The mission of Coffee House Press is to publish exciting, vital, and enduring authors of our time; to delight and inspire readers; to contribute to the cultural life of our community; and to enrich our literary heritage. By building on the best traditions of publishing and the book arts, we produce books that celebrate imagination, innovation in the craft of writing, and the many authentic voices of the American experience.

COLOPHON

Psychedelic Norway was designed at Coffee House Press, in the historic Grain Belt Brewery's Bottling House near downtown Minneapolis. The text is set in Garamond.

COFFEE HOUSE PRESS is an independent, nonprofit literary publisher. Our books are made possible through the generous support of grants and gifts from many foundations, corporate giving programs, state and federal support, and through donations from individuals who believe in the transformational power of literature. Coffee House Press receives major operating support from Amazon, the Bush Foundation, the McKnight Foundation, from the National Endowment for the Arts—a federal agency, from Target, and in part from a grant provided by the Minnesota State Arts Board through an appropriation by the Minnesota State Legislature from the State's general fund and its arts and cultural heritage fund with money from the vote of the people of Minnesota on November 4, 2008, and a grant from the Wells Fargo Foundation of Minnesota. Support for this title was received through special project support from the Jerome Foundation. Coffee House also receives support from: several anonymous donors; Suzanne Allen; Elmer L. and Eleanor J. Andersen Foundation; Around Town Agency; Patricia Beithon; Bill Berkson; the E. Thomas Binger and Rebecca Rand Fund of the Minneapolis Foundation; the Patrick and Aimee Butler Family Foundation; the Buuck Family Foundation, Ruth Dayton; Dorsey & Whitney, LLP; Mary Ebert and Paul Stembler; Chris Fischbach and Katie Dublinski; Fredrikson & Byron, P.A.; Sally French; Anselm Hollo and Jane Dalrymple-Hollo; Jeffrey Hom; Carl and Heidi Horsch; Kenneth Kahn; Alex and Ada Katz; Stephen and Isabel Keating; the Kenneth Koch Literary Estate; Kathy and Dean Koutsky; the Lenfestey Family Foundation; Carol and Aaron Mack; Mary McDermid; Sjur Midness and Briar Andresen; the Nash Foundation; the Rehael Fund of the Minneapolis Foundation; Schwegman, Lundberg & Woessner, P.A.; Kiki Smith; Jeffrey Sugerman and Sarah Schultz; Patricia Tilton; the Archie D. & Bertha H. Walker Foundation; Stu Wilson and Mel Barker; the Woessner Freeman Family Foundation; Margaret and Angus Wurtele; and many other generous individual donors.

   amazon.com

ART WORKS. MINNESOTA STATE ARTS BOARD **TARGET.**

To you and our many readers across the country, we send our thanks for your continuing support.

John recommends these Coffee House Press books

ROUGH, AND SAVAGE, BY SUN YUNG SHIN
"Shin's poems enact what happens when the violence and erasure of history collide with the poetic impulse to make meaning."
—*STAR TRIBUNE*
2013 Believer Poetry Award Finalist

THE FIRST FLAG, BY SARAH FOX
"Sarah Fox subverts the notion of a poem as a single, unified text. She uses collage, footnotes and fragmentation to create poly-vocal works with both visual and textual elements."—*STAR TRIBUNE*

HORSE, FLOWER, BIRD, BY KATE BERNHEIMER
"By turns lovely and tragic, Bernheimer's spare but captivating fables of femininity resonate like a string of sad but all-too-real and meaningful dreams. This is a collection readers won't soon forget, one that redefines the fairy tale into something wholly original." —*BOOKLIST*

NETSUKE, BY RIKKI DUCORNET
"Written in lyrical, sensuous prose, as if shrouded in a fog of humidity, *Netsuke* emerges as a character study of a man in crisis."
—*THE SEATTLE TIMES*

10 MISSISSIPPI, BY STEVE HEALEY
"What art does when it tells us awful things in ways so beautifully made creates a rip in our spirit where deeper and real truth can get in." —*DARA WIER*

WHORLED, BY ED BOK LEE
"*Whorled* is a book that believes love is like a superior kind of capital: It's a force that flows into new markets, sensing absences, and fills them, whether it's a debased kind of space or an ennobling one." —*STAR TRIBUNE*

JOHN COLBURN lives in Northeast Minneapolis. He's an editor and copublisher at Spout Press and the author of *Invisible Daughter*. With his wife, Sarah Fox, he tends the Center for Visionary Poetics. He is also a member of the improvised music collective Astronaut Cooper's Parade.